Reader's Theater Scripts

Improve Fluency, Vocabulary, and Comprehension

TEACHER RECOMMENDED • STANDARDS & RESEARCH BASED

Author

Sarah Kartchner Clark, M.A.

Publishing Credits

Dona Herweck Rice, *Editor-in-Chief*; Lee Aucoin, *Creative Director*; Don Tran, *Print Production Manager*; Conni Medina, M.A.Ed., *Editorial Director*; Jamey Acosta, *Assistant Editor*; Juan Chavolla, *Production Artist*; Corinne Burton, M.S.Ed., *Publisher*

Shell Education
5301 Oceanus Drive
Huntington Beach, CA 92649-1030
http://www.shelleducation.com

ISBN 978-1-4258-0695-8

Table of Contents

Introduction

The Connection Between Fluency and Reader's Theater

What Is Reader's Theater?

With reader's theater, students use scripts to practice for a performance. The students do not memorize their lines, and costumes and props are minimal, if used at all. The students convey the meaning of the words using their voices; therefore, interpretation of the text becomes the focus of the activity. Reader's theater gives students at all levels the motivation to practice fluency. The U.S. Department of Education's *Put Reading First* (2001) says: "Reader's theater provides readers with a legitimate reason to reread text and to practice fluency. Reader's theater also promotes cooperative interaction with peers and makes the reading task appealing."

What Is Reading Fluency?

Reading fluency is the ability to read quickly and accurately with meaning, while at the same time using vocal expression (to portray feelings and emotions of characters) and proper phrasing (timing, intonation, word emphasis). The fluent reader groups words in meaningful ways that closely resemble spoken language. Fluency is now seen as a direct connection to reading comprehension (Kuhn and Stahl 2000). It bridges the gap between word recognition and reading comprehension.

The National Reading Panel Report (National Institute of Child Health and Human Development 2000) identified five critical factors that are necessary for effective reading instruction. These factors are:

- phonemic awareness
- phonics
- fluency
- vocabulary
- comprehension

Fluency is particularly important for children first learning to read. LaBerge and Samuels (1974) state that readers have a limited amount of attention to focus on reading. Teachers notice this phenomenon when, after listening to a struggling reader, they find that the student cannot explain what he or she has just read. The struggling student has used all available concentration to decode the words and thus fails to grasp the full meaning of the text.

A student who reads fluently processes the text with more comprehension. Timothy Rasinski (1990) found that grouping words into phrases improves comprehension. When the text sounds like natural speech, students are better able to use their own knowledge and experiences to enhance comprehension.

Introduction *(cont.)*

The Connection Between Fluency and Reader's Theater *(cont.)*

How Is Fluency Developed?

Oral reading practice is required for fluency development. Building fluency takes time and develops gradually with practice. A 1979 study by Samuels supports the power of rereading as a fluency builder. In this study, students with learning problems were asked to read a passage several times. Each time the students reread the selection, their reading rate, accuracy, and comprehension increased. The most surprising finding in Samuels's study is that these students also improved on initial readings of other passages of equal or greater difficulty. Their increase in fluency transferred to new and unknown passages.

How Can Reader's Theater Develop Fluency?

Each reader's theater script includes parts for several children to read together, therefore facilitating student participation in a limited form of paired reading, another proven fluency strategy. In paired reading, a stronger reader is partnered with a struggling reader. By listening to the fluent reader, the struggling reader learns how voice, expression, and phrasing help to make sense of the words. This strategy also provides a model for the struggling reader and helps him or her to move through the text at an appropriate rate.

Reader's theater is a simple tool that supports multiple aspects of reading and nets significant gains in reading for the students. It is not only effective in developing reading fluency, it is a motivating factor that can transform a class into eager readers. It is one activity within the school day in which struggling readers do not stand out. With teacher support and repeated practice, all students can do the following:

- read their lines with accuracy and expression
- gain confidence in their own reading abilities
- enhance their listening, vocabulary development, decoding, comprehension, and speaking skills

A Note to Teachers from a Working Teacher

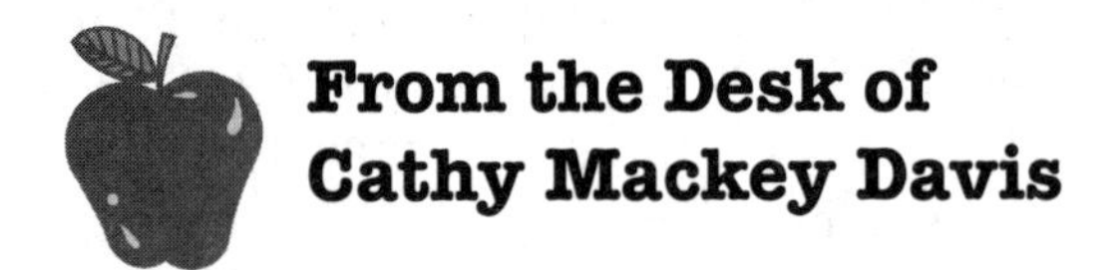

From the Desk of
Cathy Mackey Davis

This book can make a teacher's life easier and provide students with beneficial reading activities. After more than 20 years as an elementary teacher, I thought I'd seen everything come down the reading pike until I received extensive training on the five components of reading. The concept of direct instruction on fluency both surprised and impressed me.

These reader's theater scripts are designed with classroom management in mind. Each reader's theater has assigned roles for students, enabling the teacher to divide the class into small groups, which can be easily monitored. Students can develop fluency through choral reading, an effective strategy that helps students practice their reader's theater parts.

Each script in this book has its own ready-to-use, teacher-friendly lesson plan. The lesson plans cover three key components of reading: vocabulary, comprehension, and fluency. The discussion questions go beyond the literal understanding of a text in an attempt to raise the students' comprehension levels. Graphic organizers are an important part of the lessons, offering direction and bringing closure to the day's activity.

The scripts can also be an addition to classroom Literacy Work Stations. The teacher can place copies of the scripts in a Drama Station or a Fluency Station. Then students choose their parts and practice with minimal teacher intervention. The discussion questions from the lesson plans can be printed on index cards as a part of the station materials. The graphic organizers from the lessons can be enlarged on poster paper as a culminating activity for the stations.

By its very nature, reader's theater encourages students to reread and to use expression and phrasing to convey the meaning of words. It is an activity that both challenges proficient readers and motivates reluctant readers.

Cathy Mackey Davis, M.Ed.
Third Grade Teacher

Introduction *(cont.)*

Differentiation

Classrooms have evolved into diverse pools of learners—English language learners and students performing above grade level, below grade level, and on grade level. Teachers are expected to meet the diverse needs of all students in one classroom. Differentiation encompasses what is taught, how it is taught, and the products children create to show what they have learned. These categories are often referred to as content, process, and product. Teachers can keep these categories in mind as they plan instruction that will best meet the needs of their students.

Differentiating for Below-Grade-Level Students

Below-grade-level students will need help with complex concepts. They need concrete examples and models to help with comprehension. They may also need extra guidance in developing oral and written language. By receiving extra support and understanding, these students will feel more secure and have greater success.

- Model fluent reading before asking students to practice on their own.
- Allocate extra practice time for oral language activities.
- Allow for kinesthetic (hands-on) activities where appropriate. For example, students may act out the meaning of a vocabulary word.

Differentiating for Above-Grade-Level Students

All students need a firm foundation in the key vocabulary and concepts of the curriculum. Even above-grade-level students may not know much about these words or concepts before a lesson begins. The difference is that they usually learn the concepts quickly. The activities and end products can be adapted appropriately for individual students.

- Ask students to explain their reasoning for their decisions about phrasing, intonation, and expression.
- Have students design their own reader's theater scripts.

Differentiating for English Language Learners

Like all learners, English language learners need teachers who have a strong knowledge base and are committed to developing students' language. It is crucial that teachers work carefully to develop English language learners' academic vocabularies. Teachers of English language learners should keep in mind the following important principles:

- Make use of realia, concrete materials, visuals, pantomime, and other nonlinguistic representations of concepts to make input comprehensible.
- Ensure that students have ample opportunities for social interactions.
- Create a nonthreatening atmosphere that encourages students to use their new language.
- Introduce words in rich contexts that support meaning.
- Respect and draw on students' backgrounds and experiences and build connections between the known and the new.

Introduction *(cont.)*

How to Use This Book

This book includes 12 reader's theater scripts and grade-level-appropriate lessons. Within each focused lesson you will find suggestions for how to connect the script to a piece of literature and a specific content area; a vocabulary mini-lesson; activities for before, during, and after reading the script; and written and oral response questions.

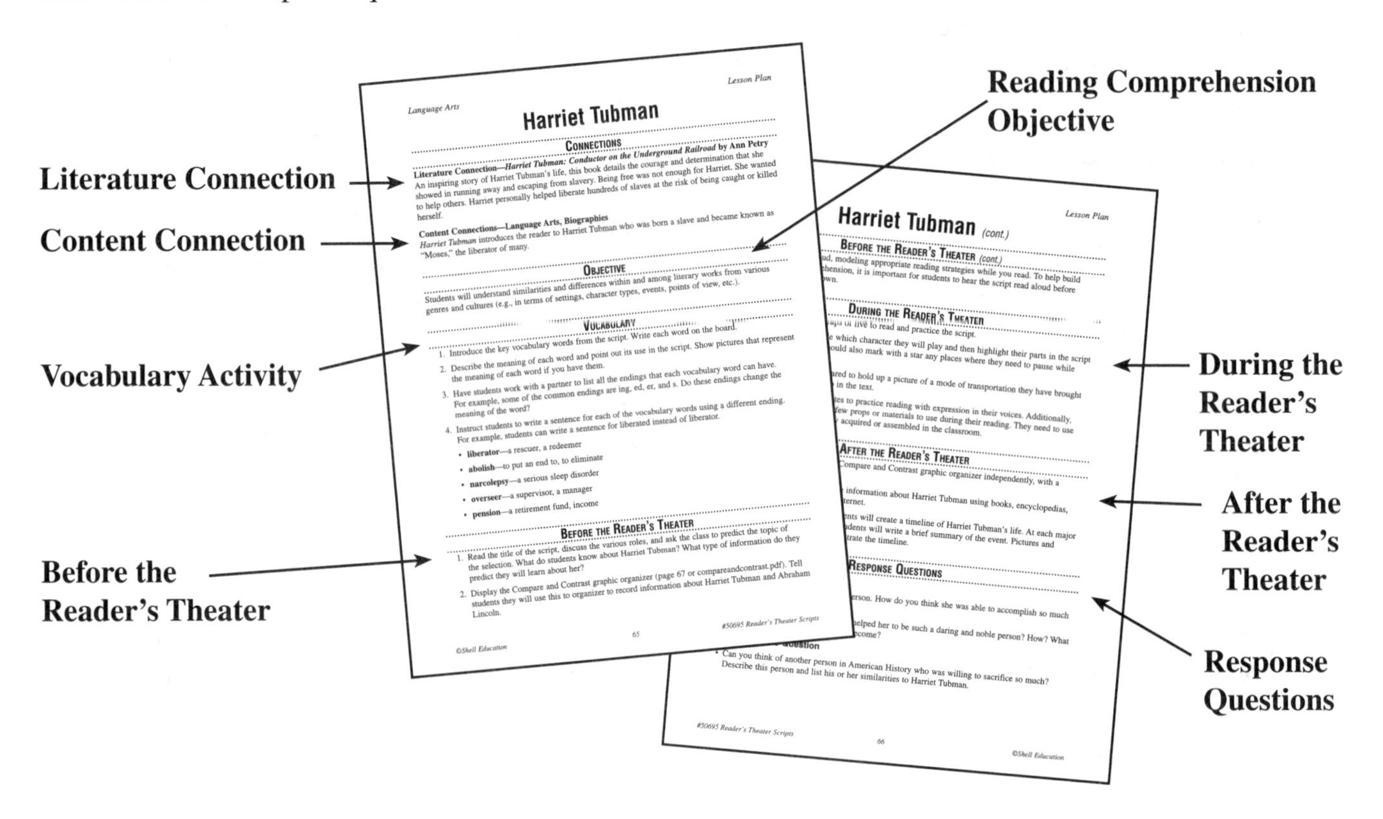

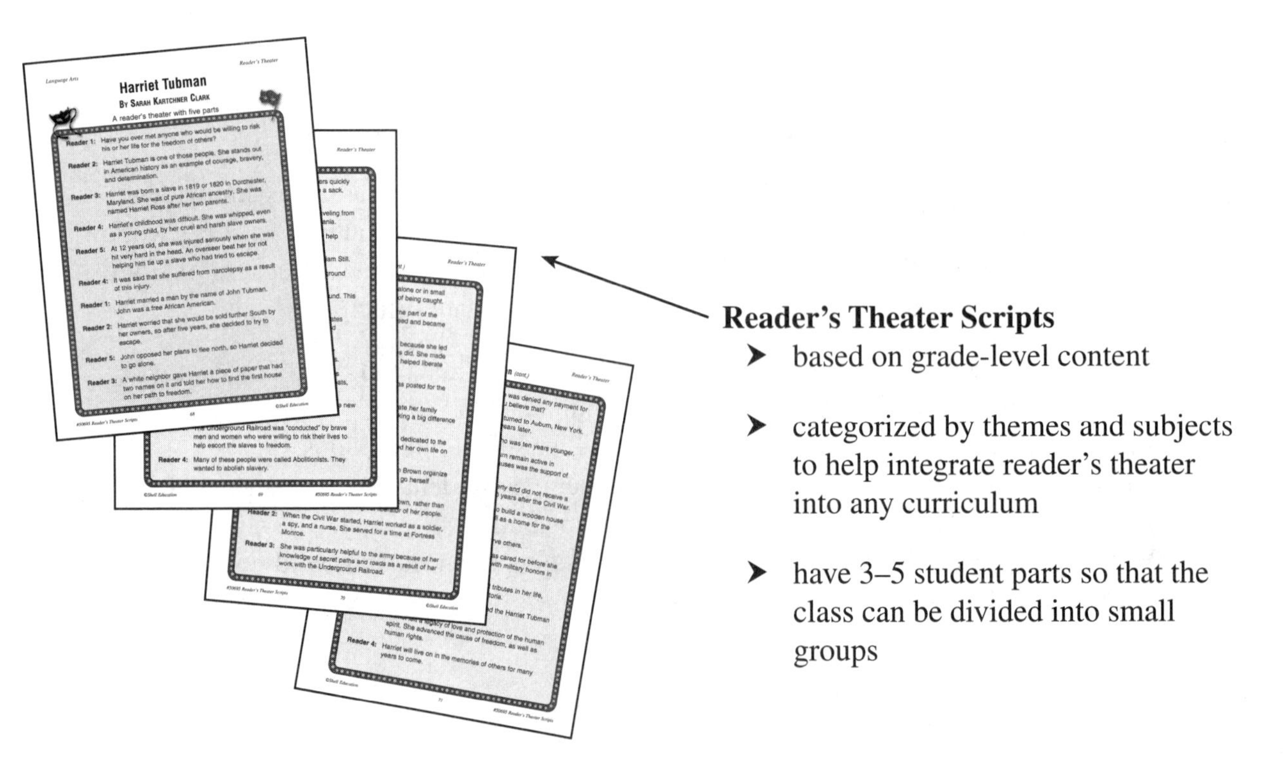

Reader's Theater Scripts

- based on grade-level content
- categorized by themes and subjects to help integrate reader's theater into any curriculum
- have 3–5 student parts so that the class can be divided into small groups

Introduction *(cont.)*

How to Use This Book *(cont.)*

Each lesson introduces a specific graphic organizer. A reproducible copy of each graphic organizer is provided in the lesson. Additionally, a PDF of each graphic organizer is available on the Teacher Resource CD.

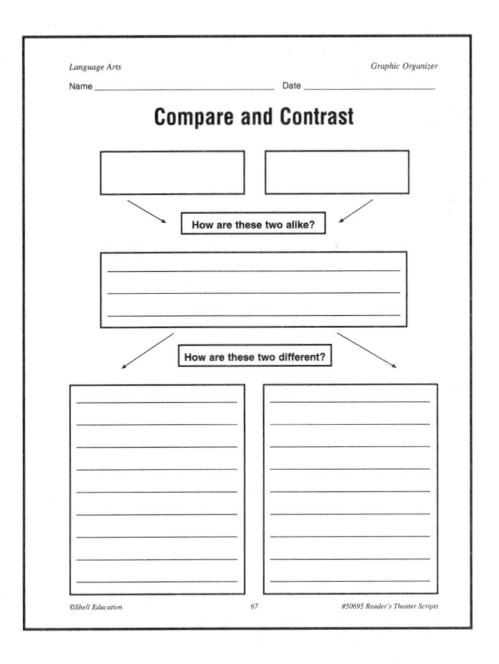

Language Arts *Graphic Organizer*

Name ______________________ Date ______________________

Compare and Contrast

How are these two alike?

How are these two different?

©Shell Education 67 #50695 Reader's Theater Scripts

Suggestions for Using and Displaying the Graphic Organizer

- **Make a transparency** of the graphic organizer and use it as a model during the lesson.
- **Use chart paper** to recreate the graphic organizer. Complete the graphic organizer as you teach the lesson.
- **Use the electronic copy** of the graphic organizer from the Teacher Resource CD to project onto the board or an interactive whiteboard.

Contents of the Teacher Resource CD

- PDF of each graphic organizer
- PDF of each script
- The contents of the CD are listed on page 102.

Introduction *(cont.)*

Standards Correlations

Shell Education is committed to producing educational materials that are research and standards based. In this effort, we have correlated all of our products to the academic standards of all 50 states, the District of Columbia, and the Department of Defense Dependent Schools.

How to Find Standards Correlations

To print a customized correlation report of this product for your state, visit our website at **http://www.shelleducation.com** and follow the on-screen directions. If you require assistance in printing correlation reports, please contact Customer Service at 1-877-777-3450.

Purpose and Intent of Standards

The No Child Left Behind legislation mandates that all states adopt academic standards that identify the skills students will learn in kindergarten through grade twelve. While many states had already adopted academic standards prior to NCLB, the legislation set requirements to ensure the standards were detailed and comprehensive.

Standards are designed to focus instruction and guide adoption of curricula. Standards are statements that describe the criteria necessary for students to meet specific academic goals. They define the knowledge, skills, and content students should acquire at each level. Standards are also used to develop standardized tests to evaluate students' academic progress.

Teachers are required to demonstrate how their lessons meet state standards. State standards are used in development of all of our products, so educators can be assured they meet the academic requirements of each state.

McREL Compendium

We use the Mid-continent Research for Education and Learning (McREL) Compendium to create standards correlations. Each year, McREL analyzes state standards and revises the compendium. By following this procedure, McREL is able to produce a general compilation of national standards. Each lesson in this product is based on one or more McREL standards. The chart on the following pages lists each standard taught in this product and the corresponding lessons.

Introduction *(cont.)*

Standards Correlations Chart

Language Arts Standards	
Lesson Title	**McREL Standard**
The Assembly Line	Summarizes and paraphrases information in texts (e.g., includes the main idea and significant supporting details of a reading selection).
World War I	Makes, confirms, and revises simple predictions about what will be found in text (e.g., uses prior knowledge and ideas presented in text, illustrations, titles, topic sentences, and key words).
The Great Depression	Uses text organizers (e.g., topic and summary sentences, graphic features) to determine the main ideas and to locate information in the text.
World War II	Summarizes and paraphrases information in texts (e.g., includes the main idea and significant supporting details of a reading selection).
Jim Thorpe	Summarizes and paraphrases information in texts (e.g., includes the main idea and significant supporting details of a reading selection).
Abraham Lincoln	Summarizes and paraphrases information in texts (e.g., includes the main idea and significant supporting details of a reading selection).
Madame Marie Curie	Uses text organizers (e.g., topic and summary sentences, graphic features) to determine the main ideas and to locate information in the text.
Harriet Tubman	Understands similarities and differences within and among literary works from various genres and cultures (e.g., in terms of settings, character types, events, point of view, roles of natural phenomena).
Earthquakes	Summarizes and paraphrases information in texts (e.g., includes the main idea and significant supporting details of a reading selection).
Space Exploration	Summarizes and paraphrases information in texts (e.g., includes the main idea and significant supporting details of a reading selection).
Plant Life	Summarizes and paraphrases information in texts (e.g., includes the main idea and significant supporting details of a reading selection).
Electricity	Summarizes and paraphrases information in texts (e.g., includes the main idea and significant supporting details of a reading selection).

Introduction *(cont.)*

Standards Correlations Chart *(cont.)*

Vocabulary Standards	
Lesson Title	**McREL Standard**
All scripts	Use a variety of context clues to decode unknown words (e.g., draws on earlier reading, reads ahead).
All scripts	Understands level-appropriate reading vocabulary (e.g., synonyms, antonyms, homophones, multi-meaning words).

Fluency Standards	
Lesson Title	**McREL Standard**
All scripts	Uses a variety of nonverbal communication skills (e.g., eye contact, gestures, facial expressions, posture).
All scripts	Uses a variety of verbal communication skills (e.g., projection, tone, volume, rate, articulation, pace, phrasing).

Introduction *(cont.)*

Tips on Reader's Theater

By Aaron Shepard

Mumble, mumble,
Stop and stumble.
Pages turn and readers fumble.

If this sounds like a description of your reader's theater efforts, try giving your readers the following tips. First, have your readers follow these instructions—individually or in a group—to prepare their scripts and get familiar with their parts.

Preparing	• Highlight your parts in your copy of the script. Mark only the words you will say—not your character's name or stage directions. • Underline the words that tell about anything you'll need to act out. • Read through your part aloud. If you're a character, think about how that character would sound. How does your character feel? Can you speak as if you were feeling that way? • Stand up and read through the script again. If you're a character, try out faces and movements. Would your character stand or move in a special way? Can you do that?
Rehearsing	• Hold your script at a steady height, but make sure it doesn't hide your face. • Speak with feeling. • S-l-o-w d-o-w-n. Say each syl-la-ble clear-ly. • TALK LOUDLY! You have to be heard in the back row. • While you speak, try to look up often. Don't just look at your script. • The narrators are important even when the audience isn't looking at you. You control the story! Be sure to give the characters enough time to do what they must. And remember that you're talking to the audience, not to yourself. • Characters, you give the story life! Remember to be your character even when you're not speaking, and be sure to react to the other characters.
Performing	• If the audience laughs, stop speaking until they can hear you again. • If someone talks in the audience, don't pay attention. • If someone walks into the room, don't look at them. • If you make a mistake, pretend it was right. • If a reader forgets to read his or her part, don't signal to the reader, just skip over it or make something up.

The Assembly Line

Connections

Literature Connection—*How Henry Ford Built a Legend* by David Weitzman

This book shares the amazing story of Henry Ford and his Model T, a new invention that gave people the ability to be mobile for the first time. This could not have happened without the moving assembly line, which was created by Ford. The theme throughout this script focuses on trying new ideas and pushing the limits.

Content Connections—Social Studies, U.S. History

This reader's theater takes students back in time to the birth of the assembly line when the roar of machines and new inventions filled the air. Streets that were once crowded with horses and buggies were now filled with the new Model T Ford cars. The assembly line increased the pace of life and allowed more people mobility.

Objective

Students will summarize and paraphrase information in texts (e.g., include the main idea and significant supporting details of a reading selection).

Vocabulary

1. Introduce the key vocabulary words from the script. Write each word on the board. Read each word aloud.
2. Describe the meaning of each word and point out its use in the script. Show pictures that represent the meaning of each word if you have them.
3. Ask students to make word associations for the selected vocabulary words. Then ask questions about linking other words with one of the vocabulary words. For example, a word association question for *consumer* might be, "Which word goes with buyer and money?" (*consumer*)
   - **assemble**—to build or construct
   - **apprentice**—a novice, trainee, or learner
   - **mechanized**—automatic or programmed; using machinery to operate or perform
   - **conveyor**—a moving belt that transports objects
   - **consumer**—a customer or buyer
   - **revolutionized**—transformed, altered, or changed in a major way

Before the Reader's Theater

1. Read the title of the script and discuss the topic of the reader's theater. Ask if anyone knows about the moving assembly line. Does anyone know how the automobile was invented? Does anyone know the inventor who is credited with mass producing cars?

The Assembly Line *(cont.)*

Before the Reader's Theater *(cont.)*

2. Display the What's the Main Idea? graphic organizer (page 16 or whatsthemainidea.pdf) and explain to students that it is a tool for taking notes about the main idea of a reading selection. Demonstrate its use by reading the first two lines of the script and selecting the important words for the graphic organizer. The class will complete the organizer together after reading the script.
3. Read the script aloud, modeling appropriate reading strategies while you read. To help build fluency and comprehension, it is important for students to hear the script read aloud before practicing on their own.

During the Reader's Theater

1. Divide the class into groups of five to read and practice the script.
2. Students need to decide which character they will play and then highlight their parts in the script (Readers 1–5). They should also mark with a star any places where they need to pause while reading.
3. Give students a few minutes to practice reading with expression in their voices. Additionally, students may decide on a few props or materials to use during their reading. They need to use materials that can be easily acquired or assembled in the classroom.
4. After they have finished practicing, have each group perform the reader's theater for the rest of the class. You may also want them to perform for another class.

After the Reader's Theater

1. Give each student a copy of What's the Main Idea? graphic organizer to complete independently or with a partner.
2. Have students conduct an Internet search for more information about the assembly line and Henry Ford.
3. Have students write a summary of what they learned about Henry Ford and the assembly line. Remind students to include the key details from the script.

Response Questions

Group Discussion Questions

- How did the assembly line change the way things were made or built? Why do you think it is important to learn about our nation's history?

Written Response Question

- How do you think the lessons learned about Henry Ford and the assembly line might change your future? Your response should be both creative and specific.

Name______________________________ Date ________________________

What's the Main Idea?

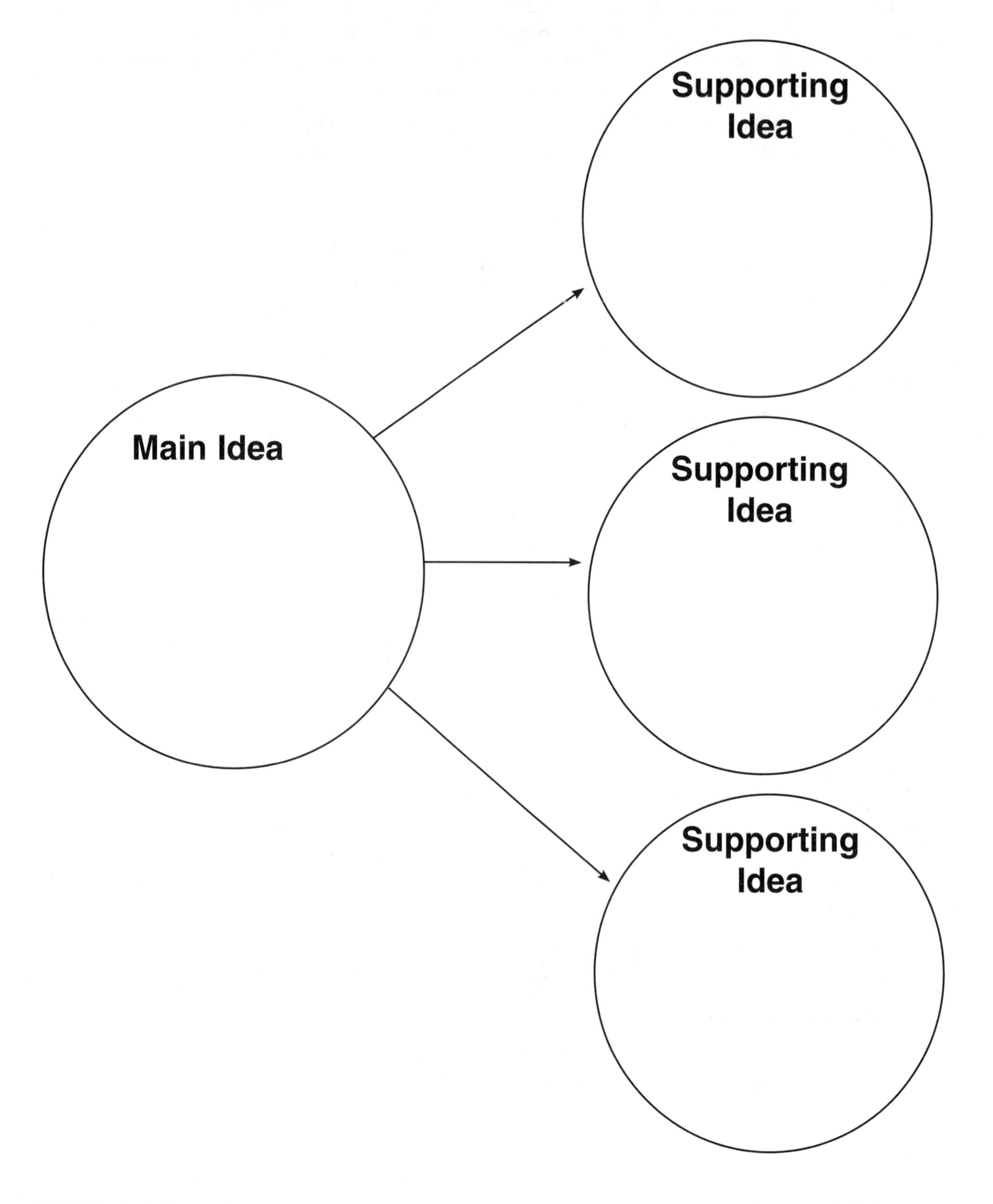

The Assembly Line

By Sarah Kartchner Clark

A reader's theater with five parts

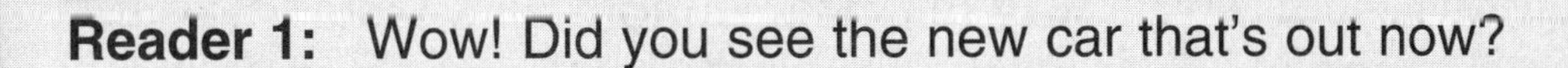

Reader 1: Wow! Did you see the new car that's out now?

Reader 5: Yes, I sure did. How fast do you think it can go?

Reader 3: It's not the speed that's so amazing.

Reader 1: What's amazing is how much cars have changed.

Reader 2: That's right. The first car was very different from cars today.

Reader 4: The moving assembly line was an important process that led to rapid change in the design of cars.

Reader 5: That's right. Henry Ford invented the moving assembly line.

Reader 1: We all know Henry Ford built Ford cars, but what did he have to do with the moving assembly line?

Reader 4: Let's start at the beginning of the story. Henry Ford was born on July 30, 1863, in Dearborn, Michigan to a wealthy farming family.

Reader 2: But farming did not interest Henry. When he was only 16, Henry left home to work as an apprentice machinist.

Reader 3: Over the next few years, Henry Ford improved his skills.

Reader 4: In 1891, he began work with the Edison Engineering Company. Ford used his work experiences to build on his inventions and ideas.

Reader 2: In 1903, Ford opened the Ford Motor Company.

The Assembly Line *(cont.)*

Reader 3: The company could only produce two or three cars per day. It took a group of two or three men to build each car.

Reader 5: The demand for the Model T was so great that Ford needed to find a way to produce more cars faster.

Reader 2: Finally, in 1913, Ford changed the way we worked by changing the way the assembly line worked.

Reader 4: The assembly line consisted of workers walking to the car or product and assembling the needed parts.

Reader 5: It took a lot of time to assemble a car this way.

Reader 1: Ford invented the mechanized conveyor belt, which brought the car to the workers.

Reader 3: The workers stayed in one place as the belt moved past them carrying the car. Thus, the continuous assembly line was born.

Reader 1: Each worker added his part to the car, and then the conveyor belt took the car to the next worker.

Reader 2: A lot of time was saved because of this conveyor belt.

Reader 4: Parts were also brought to the worker on the conveyor belt.

Reader 5: The motorized assembly line was a huge success.

Reader 2: Ford Motor Company became the largest car manufacturer in the world.

Reader 4: So, how did the assembly line change the way other people worked?

The Assembly Line *(cont.)*

Reader 1: People from all over the world came to Detroit to learn the secrets of Ford's moving assembly line.

Reader 5: Mass production for a variety of products was now possible for factories all over the world.

Reader 3: The moving assembly line revolutionized the way companies made products.

Reader 2: Factories still use assembly lines today.

Reader 1: Factories use assembly lines to mass-produce everything, from the food we eat to the clothes we wear.

Reader 4: Without the moving assembly line, every product would be made at a much slower rate.

Reader 3: What else did the moving assembly line do?

Reader 5: The quicker assembly line cut manufacturing costs as well.

Reader 4: So the company could lower prices and offer less expensive products for the consumer.

Reader 2: All these changes sound like great things!

Reader 1: They sure do. These changes revolutionized the American economy.

Reader 5: Henry Ford used the ideas of others to create a new idea. It pays to learn from others and to share ideas.

Reader 4: Learning from others is valuable. America's history is filled with people who learned from others to create good ideas.

Reader 3: I can't wait to see what the next new idea will be!

World War I

Connections

Literature Connection—*After the Dancing Days* by Margaret Rostkowski
After the Dancing Days is a fictionalized, but historically accurate, snapshot of life in the United States during World War I. Annie learns the realities of war following the end of The Great War through her friendship with a veteran, and she discovers the truth about her uncle's heroism. She learns of sacrifices made both at home and abroad.

Content Connections—Social Studies, U.S. History
World War I takes the reader beyond the borders of the United States during World War I.

Objective

Students will make, confirm, and revise simple predictions about will be found in the text (e.g., use prior knowledge and ideas presented in the text, illustrations, titles, topic sentences, and key words).

Vocabulary

1. Introduce the key vocabulary words from the script. Write each word on the board. Read each word aloud.
2. Describe the meaning of each word and point out its use in the script. Show pictures that represent the meaning of each word if you have them.
3. Have students play a game of quick draw. Ask each student to come up to the front of the room and draw an illustration for the word as other students try to guess the word that is being drawn. The student who guesses the word correctly gets to come up and draw the next vocabulary word.
   - **assassinated**—murdered or killed by another person, often for political reasons
   - **entangled**—entwined or snarled
   - **trench**—a ditch or dugout
   - **epidemics**—plagues or diseases
   - **morale**—confidence, spirit, or self-esteem

Before the Reader's Theater

1. Read the title of the script and ask the class to make predictions about this reader's theater. Is it fiction or nonfiction? Why do they think so? Does anyone know which countries were involved in World War I?
2. Display the K-W-L Chart graphic organizer (page 22 or kwlchart.pdf). Demonstrate its use by filling in a few examples of prior knowledge about World War I under the "Know" column of the chart. Then fill in information for the "Want to Know" column. The class will fill in the information in the "Learned" column after reading the script.

World War I *(cont.)*

Before the Reader's Theater *(cont.)*

3. Read the script aloud, modeling appropriate reading strategies while you read. To help build fluency and comprehension, it is important for students to hear the script read aloud before practicing on their own.

During the Reader's Theater

1. Divide the class into groups of four to read and practice the script.
2. Students need to decide which character they will play and then highlight their parts in the script (Readers 1–4). They should also mark with a star any places where they need to pause while reading.
3. Give students a few minutes to practice reading with expression in their voices. Additionally, students may decide on a few props or materials to use during their reading. They need to use materials that can be easily acquired or assembled in the classroom.
4. After they have finished practicing, have each group perform the reader's theater for the rest of the class. You may also want them to perform for another class.

After the Reader's Theater

1. As a class, complete the K-W-L Chart.
2. Have students conduct organized research about World War I using a variety of sources, including books, reference books, magazines, encyclopedias, and the Internet.
3. After gathering sufficient information, students will write a research report sharing their findings. Make sure students list the sources of information they used in a references cited page.

Response Questions

Group Discussion Questions

- Why was World War I also known as the Great War?
- What are some of the lessons that were learned from the Great War?
- Why was there a World War II if these lessons were learned?

Written Response Question

- How do you think countries can live together peacefully? What suggestions do you have for the leaders of countries today?

Name ______________________________ Date ______________________

K-W-L Chart

K	W	L

World War I

By Sarah Kartchner Clark

A reader's theater with four parts

All: Beep! Beep! Beep! Beep!

Reader 1: This just in! The Lusitania has been hit!

Reader 2: That's right. Official word is that as a result of this, the United States has broken off relations with Germany.

Reader 3: It's February 1917, and the Great War has been going on in Europe now for almost three years. Back to you in the studio.

Reader 4: Tensions have been rising in Europe for many years.

Reader 1: It finally came to a head in 1914 when a Serbian nationalist assassinated Austrian Archduke Francis Ferdinand and his wife in Sarajevo.

Reader 2: This plunged the countries of Europe into what has been known as the Great War.

Reader 3: The two sides of the war are known as the Allies and the Central Powers.

Reader 4: And which are the countries that make up the Allies and the Central Powers?

Reader 1: The Allies consist mainly of Britain, France, Russia, Italy, and Japan.

Reader 2: The Central Powers consist of Germany, Turkey, and Austria-Hungary.

Reader 4: Once the United States engaged the Germans, were they on the side of the Allies?

World War I *(cont.)*

Reader 3: That's correct. Word is that the United States will join the war in the next few months.

All: Beep! Beep! Beep! Beep!

Reader 1: It has been a few months since we last reported. Word is that the United States officially declared war on Germany on April 6, 1917.

Reader 2: Submarine warfare has reached its peak in the North Atlantic Ocean.

Reader 3: American troops have landed in France.

Reader 1: The troops have been able to hold off the German offensive in Chateau-Thierry. Back to you in the studio.

Reader 4: Thanks. So how are things looking? Reports have been filed here saying that French and American troops stopped a critical German attack outside of Paris in July and parts of August.

Reader 2: That information seems to be correct.

Reader 3: This war has definitely been different than all other wars.

Reader 4: Why is that?

Reader 3: There are several reasons, but one of them is that so many countries have been entangled in this web of war.

Reader 1: Groups of countries are fighting groups of other countries—thus, the name "the Great War." It's greater than any other war that's been fought.

Reader 2: This war has also been characterized by trench warfare.

Reader 4: What is trench warfare?

World War I *(cont.)*

Reader 2: Trench warfare is when each army, on opposing sides, has dug long, deep trenches in the ground.

Reader 3: The soldiers sleep, eat, and fight against the enemy in these trenches.

All: Beep! Beep! Beep! Beep!

Reader 1: This report is coming to you live from Europe.

Reader 2: A unified allied command is pushing hard against the German command. The German counterattack, known as the second Battle of Marne, was stopped, preventing the Germans from entering Paris.

Reader 3: The Allied attack continued until German resources and morale collapsed.

Reader 4: So what is the status of the war now?

Reader 1: The ball is in Germany's court. Will they back down? Or, will they continue to fight?

Reader 2: Rumors here say the Germans will indeed surrender and this Great War will end. We'll keep you posted.

All: Beep! Beep! Beep! Beep!

Reader 4: We have just received word that the war in Europe has ended. Our reporters are now standing by in the field with new information.

Reader 3: Hi. We are standing on soil that was once filled with armies and weapons. The ground has been destroyed. There is little left of the landscape except mud and trenches.

Reader 1: Germany asked for an armistice, or cease-fire.

World War I *(cont.)*

Reader 2: The Great War ended on November 11, 1918, at 11:00 A.M. President Woodrow Wilson of the United States proposed a program called the Fourteen Points.

Reader 4: The Fourteen Points is a peace program. These points outline what is necessary to keep peace in Europe and prevent another war.

Reader 1: The points are very idealistic. After being changed and weakened, they led to the formation of the League of Nations and the Treaty of Versailles.

Reader 3: The signing of the Treaty of Versailles ended the Great War.

Reader 1: Although the United States has not joined the League of Nations, the League is organized to resolve disputes between countries.

Reader 3: The Treaty of Versailles, along with other treaties, has changed the map of Europe, creating new boundaries for many countries.

Reader 4: Can you tell us the costs of this war?

Reader 2: The cost of the Great War is difficult to assess. Some say that as many as 10 million people died and 20 million were wounded.

Reader 1: Starvation and epidemics have increased the death count.

Reader 3: The current attitude in Europe seems to be one that despises war and intends to neutralize tension between countries to prevent another war like the Great War. Back to you.

Reader 4: There you have it, ladies and gentlemen. The end of the Great War. Let's hope this truly is the end of all wars.

The Great Depression

Connections

Literature Connection—*Out of the Dust* by Karen Hesse
Out of the Dust is the story of 14-year-old Billie Jo. Living in Oklahoma during the Dust Bowl in the midst of the Great Depression, Billie Jo learns what sacrifice means. Her mother dies in a serious accident, which compounds Billie Jo's feelings of who she is and where she is going.

Content Connections—Social Studies, U.S. History
The Great Depression takes the reader inside the home of a family struggling to survive when everyone is without work. This family confronts the challenges that were common during the Great Depression.

Objective

Students use text organizers (e.g., topic and summary sentences, graphic features) to determine the main ideas and to locate information in text.

Vocabulary

1. Introduce the key vocabulary words from the script. Write each word on the board. Read each word aloud.
2. Describe the meaning of each word and point out its use in the script.
3. Have students work in small groups to create visual representations for the vocabulary words. Put students into groups, and give each group a piece of chart paper. Assign one word to each group. Then have each group create a visual representation for its assigned word. Allow time for each group to share its poster with the class.
    - **ignorance**—not having knowledge, unlearned
    - **plantation**—a large estate used for agriculture
    - **prosper**—to do well, to show growth
    - **success**—an accomplished goal
    - **trade**—a job requiring a skill

Before the Reader's Theater

1. Read the title of the script and ask the class to make predictions about this reader's theater. Is it fiction or nonfiction? Why do they thinks so? Is it fiction or nonfiction? Ask if the students know about the Great Depression. Are any students familiar with the Dust Bowl?
2. Display the Main Idea graphic organizer (page 29 or mainidea.pdf). Ask students to write the main idea of the reader's theater script at the top of the organizer. Example: Families had to work together during the Great Depression.
3. As students read the script, they should record details about the Great Depression

The Great Depression *(cont.)*

Before the Reader's Theater *(cont.)*

4. Read the script aloud, modeling appropriate reading strategies while you read. To help build fluency and comprehension, it is important for students to hear the script read aloud before practicing on their own.

During the Reader's Theater

1. Divide the class into groups of five to read and practice the script.
2. Students need to decide which character they will play and then highlight their parts in the script (Readers 1–5). They should also mark with a star any places where they need to pause while reading.
3. Give students a few minutes to practice reading with expression in their voices. Additionally, students may decide on a few props or materials to use during their reading. They need to use materials that can be easily acquired or assembled in the classroom.
4. After they have finished practicing, have each group perform the reader's theater for the rest of the class. You may also want them to perform for another class.

After the Reader's Theater

1. As a class, complete the Main Idea graphic organizer.
2. Ask students to conduct an interview with someone who lived during the Great Depression. Have students create a list of questions prior to the interview so that they will be prepared.
3. After gathering sufficient information, students will write a report sharing their findings. The report should compare and contrast growing up during the Great Depression to growing up today.

Response Questions

Group Discussion Questions

- What caused the Great Depression? Could a Great Depression happen again?
- What are some of the lessons we learned from the Great Depression?
- How do you think families survived such difficult challenges? Can you think of challenges that your family has had to face?

Written Response Question

- What would you do if your parents lost their jobs? What could you do to help make ends meet?

Name ______________________________ Date ____________________

Main Idea

Main Idea

Detail

Detail

Detail

Detail

The Great Depression

By Sarah Kartchner Clark

A reader's theater with five parts

Reader 1: Oh man! Not green beans again!

Reader 2: Green beans aren't that bad!

Reader 3: That's right. We are lucky to have green beans. They are healthy and they are very hard to come by these days.

Reader 4: What does "come by" mean?

Reader 3: It means that green beans are hard to find. We are in a depression and food is very scarce.

Reader 2: Everyone keeps talking about a depression. Does that mean everyone is feeling sad?

Reader 3: No. What they mean is that the economy is in a depression. People don't have much money or food, and there is no work.

Reader 1: I heard that Mr. Wilson lost his job yesterday.

Reader 3: Yes, he did. We hope he can find work in the area or the Wilsons will move to California like everybody else.

Reader 2: Why is everybody moving to California? Doesn't California have a depression too?

Reader 4: Maybe people want to go where beans are plentiful and food is available.

Reader 3: People are trying to find work so they can feed their families. California isn't experiencing a drought like we are here in the Dust Bowl. And besides, there are crops to pick and fruit to harvest in California. Now, let's set the table before Dad comes home.

The Great Depression *(cont.)*

Reader 1: There he is now. I see him walking up the steps.

Reader 2: Don't worry. We will set the table, but I just can't eat any of those green beans. They look gross.

Reader 5: Hello, I'm home.

Reader 3: Hi, Dear. Any luck today finding a job?

Reader 5: Not today, but I hear that a job may be available at Henry's Meatpacking Plant.

Reader 4: Why can't you go back to your job at the bank?

Reader 5: The bank closed and there are no jobs there anymore.

Reader 1: But the bank is still there. I see it every time I ride my bike past the place.

Reader 5: The building is still there, but the bank is closed. The sign is out front, but nobody works there anymore.

Reader 3: The bank closed like many other businesses after the stock market crashed in 1929.

Reader 5: That's right. I wasn't the only one to lose my job. Thousands of people lost their jobs. All the businesses that went bankrupt had to close.

Reader 2: Are people moving to California to try to get jobs?

Reader 1: Well, that makes sense.

Reader 3: It does make sense. Many of the people leaving are farmers.

Reader 4: Many of them lost their farms to the drought and what has become known as the Dust Bowl.

The Great Depression *(cont.)*

Reader 3: People can't grow anything in all that dust!

Reader 5: That's right. No crops can grow here, but people say there are many crops growing in California.

Reader 2: I'm really going to miss Sue if she moves.

Reader 1: Are we going to have to move to California?

Reader 5: I hope not. I'm hoping I can get a job here in town. Mr. Riley says he's willing to keep me as long as he's got the money to pay me. The problem is that it's only a part-time job. If that job at the meatpacking plant works out, it should help us pay our bills.

Reader 3: Come on. Let's eat. We can talk about this over dinner.

Reader 2: You mean over green beans.

Reader 4: So why does everyone have to lose their jobs?

Reader 1: They don't do it on purpose.

Reader 5: No, they don't do it on purpose.

Reader 2: Sue said something called the stock market crashed.

Reader 3: It did.

Reader 1: So why didn't they just pick up the pieces and put it back together?

Reader 5: The stock market isn't made of glass. The stock market is a place where people buy and sell stock.

Reader 4: People buy stock and when the price goes up, they sell it and make money.

Reader 2: That sounds like a good idea.

The Great Depression *(cont.)*

Reader 3: It was a good idea until people began borrowing money to buy more and more stocks.

Reader 2: Even if they couldn't afford it?

Reader 5: Yes. They borrowed even if they couldn't afford it and that's what caused the problem.

Reader 3: Soon, the price of stocks stopped rising and the prices began to fall.

Reader 5: People lost money. Some people lost everything they owned.

Reader 1: So people were spending money they didn't have?

Reader 5: Yes.

Reader 3: When everyone started losing money, they could no longer run their businesses, and people lost their jobs.

Reader 4: And if people lose their jobs, they can't buy food and they have to eat green beans from the pantry.

Reader 5: That's right. Mmmm! Don't these green beans taste good?

Reader 1: It's not bad if you consider what we could be eating.

Reader 2: My friend Jean said that her family is going to have boarders live with them. What's a boarder?

Reader 3: Many families are taking in boarders. A boarder lives in a room in your house. The boarder pays the family rent to live there.

Reader 2: It's a way for families to make some money. I just wish we had the space to take in one or two boarders.

The Great Depression *(cont.)*

Reader 4: We could sleep outside on a bedroll. The boarders could have our room.

Reader 1: You just don't want to clean our room.

Reader 2: It's too cold to sleep outside.

Reader 5: Yes, it's much too cold right now to be sleeping outside. We'll work things out.

All: We always do.

Reader 3: One good thing about this depression is that people are trying to help one another.

Reader 1: When we help others, we feel better, and our own situation doesn't look so bad.

Reader 4: I'd be willing to share some of my green beans.

All: WHAT?

Reader 4: Just trying to help.

Reader 5: Thanks. I read in the paper today that President Roosevelt is organizing a program to put people to work building roads and other public projects.

Reader 3: Work is just the thing people need right now.

Reader 2: I know what I need right now.

Reader 1: What do you need, Sally?

Reader 2: I need somebody to pass me the green beans!

World War II

Connections

Literature Connection—*Early Sunday Morning: The Pearl Harbor Diary of Amber Billows, Hawaii, 1941* by Barry Denenberg
This book shares the details of how the United States entered the Second World War. Japan attacked Pearl Harbor on December 7, 1941. Life in the United States immediately changed. Supporting the troops became a priority. Families went without many items, and victory gardens dotted the country as a means of support.

Content Connections—Social Studies, U.S. History
World War II gives the reader a glimpse into life during World War II. The grandchildren ask their grandparents what it was like to fight in the war and to live during that time period in U.S. history.

Objective

Students will summarize and paraphrase information in texts (e.g., include the main idea and significant supporting details of a reading selection).

Vocabulary

1. Introduce the key vocabulary words from the script. Write each word on the board.
2. Describe the meaning of each word and point out its use in the script.
3. Challenge the class to a game of team charades. Divide the class into small groups. Assign each group a vocabulary word to act out for the class. Give each group three minutes to decide how to demonstrate its assigned word. Challenge the other groups to guess the word.
   - **ration**—a portion, an allowance, or a quota
   - **mobilize**—to assemble or gather together
   - **pivotal**—important, decisive, or fundamental
   - **devastating**—damaging, harmful, or dreadful
   - **allies**—partners, associates, friends, or helpers

Before the Reader's Theater

1. Read the title of the script. Ask students to make predictions about this reader's theater. Is it fiction or nonfiction? Why do they think so? What do students know about World War II? How can this information be helpful while reading and presenting this reader's theater?
2. Display the Idea Web graphic organizer (page 37 or ideaweb.pdf). Use this graphic to organize the information students gather on World War II. In the large, middle circle, write the key concept or idea. In the smaller circles surrounding the middle circle, record notes and information gathered on this topic. Be sure to group similar notes and ideas together in one circle. Each circle represents a different topic or idea that refers back to the key concept.

World War II *(cont.)*

Before the Reader's Theater *(cont.)*

3. Read the script aloud, modeling appropriate reading strategies while you read. To help build fluency and comprehension, it is important for students to hear the script read aloud before practicing on their own.

During the Reader's Theater

1. Divide the class into groups of four to read and practice the script.
2. Students need to decide which character they will play and then highlight their parts in the script (Readers 1–4). They should also mark with a star any places where they need to pause while reading.
3. Give students a few minutes to practice reading with expression in their voices. Additionally, students may decide on a few props or materials to use during their reading. They need to use materials that can be easily acquired or assembled in the classroom.
4. After they have finished practicing, have each group perform the reader's theater for the rest of the class. You may also want them to perform for another class.

After the Reader's Theater

1. As a class, finish filling in the Idea Web graphic organizer, assisting students as needed.
2. Have students research World War II, using a variety of sources, including books, reference materials, magazines, encyclopedias, and the Internet.
3. After gathering sufficient information, students will write a fictional letter to the president of the United States that lists the lessons learned from World War II, and how these lessons can be useful in making foreign policy decisions today.
4. Ask students to write a summary of what they have learned and list suggestions for the future.

Response Questions

Group Discussion Questions

- What do you think about the use of the atomic bomb during World War II?
- Why do you think Hitler had so much power and influence over people and countries?

Written Response Question

- What do you think are reasons that a country may be justified in going to war? What are reasons not to go to war?

Name________________________________ Date ____________________________

Idea Web

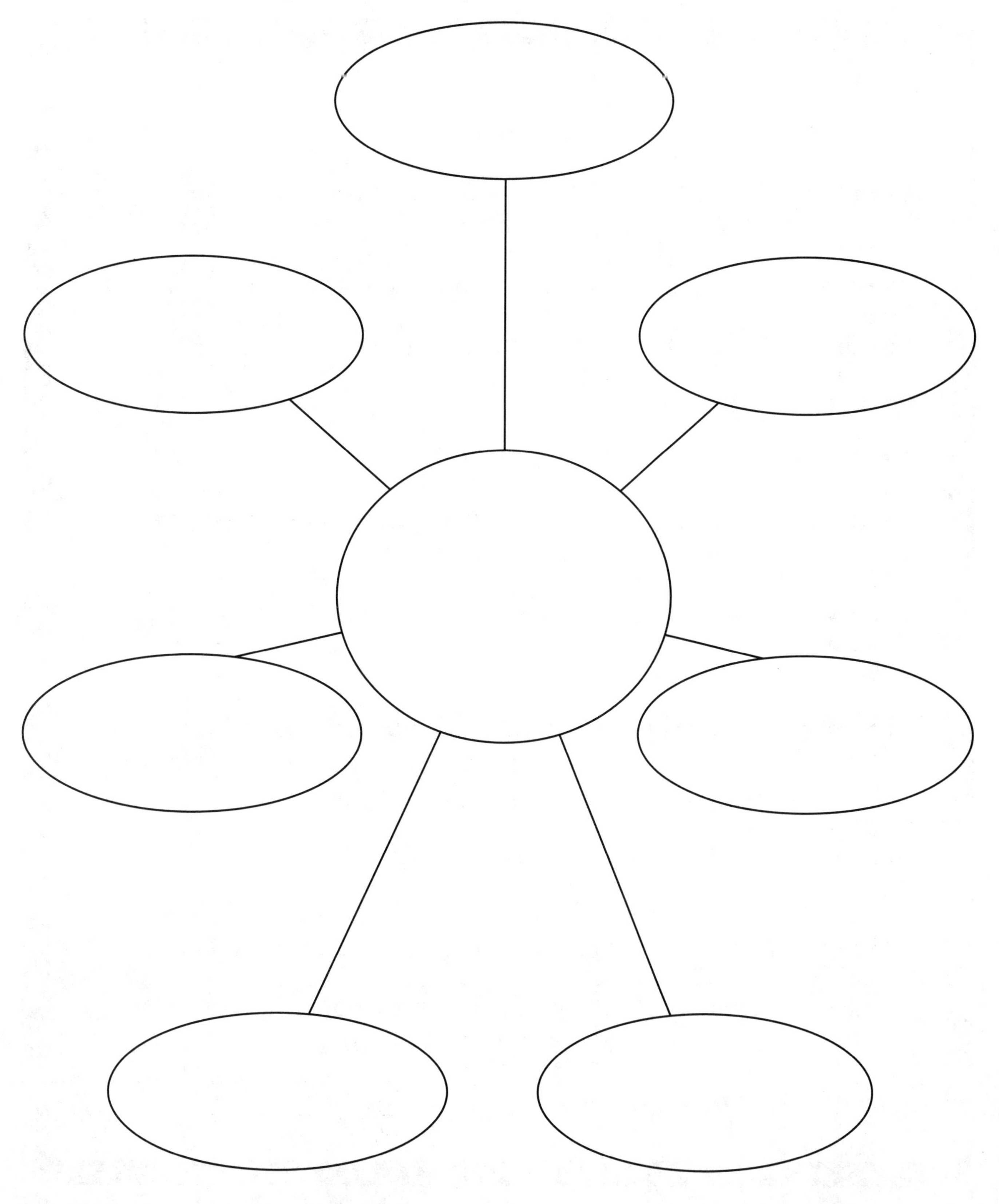

World War II

By Sarah Kartchner Clark

A reader's theater with four parts

Reader 1: Hey, what is that book you are reading?

Reader 3: Oh, it's a book about World War II.

Reader 4: Cool! Can you tell us some stories about what life was like during World War II?

Reader 3: Sure. We can tell you a story about World War II.

Reader 1: Tell us about one of the battle stories.

Reader 2: There I was...

Reader 4: Don't make it too gorey.

Reader 2: I'll try not to, but most of the battle stories have some blood in them.

Reader 1: Yeah!

Reader 3: Sit with me.

Reader 2: There I was...The weekend before I left to report to duty, I got married. She was the most beautiful bride. Marrying her was the best decision I ever made.

Reader 4: Wasn't it hard to leave her?

Reader 3: It was very difficult for us, but it was hard for most people back then. We wanted to support our country.

Reader 2: Knowing my wife was at home supporting me gave me the strength to do the things I had to do.

Reader 1: So what did you do?

World War II *(cont.)*

Reader 2: I was a member of the 36th Division out of Texas. We mobilized on November 25, 1940. I remember it like it was yesterday.

Reader 1: Where were you when you mobilized?

Reader 2: We were in Camp Bowie, Texas. We were in combat for 19 months and fought five major campaigns.

Reader 2: The enemy was everywhere. I was scared to death, but that adrenaline kicks in and you just do what you have to do. I shot at anything that moved. It's amazing that I made it home alive.

Reader 4: So, what were you doing while he was fighting the war?

Reader 3: I was working. It's the hardest work I've ever done. We worked night and day. In the factories, women took the places of all the men fighting at war. Approximately six million women went to work during the war.

Reader 1: What did they do?

Reader 3: Women were builders, welders, factory workers, machinists—anything! Rosie the Riveter was our mascot. We were supporting the troops across the sea. It was our way of helping fight the war.

Reader 2: Women weren't the only ones supporting the troops. The kids were, too.

Reader 4: What did the kids do?

Reader 3: The kids planted victory gardens and sacrificed many comforts.

Reader 1: What kinds of comforts?

World War II *(cont.)*

Reader 3: Certain goods became scarce. The government put a ration on meat, butter, shoes, tires, and gasoline.

Reader 4: What is a ration?

Reader 2: A ration limits the amount that a person can get of certain items, such as butter, meat, or other necessities.

Reader 1: Did rationing make the adults and kids mad?

Reader 3: Oh, no. They were happy to help support the troops and the United States.

Reader 4: So, how did the United States get involved in this war anyway?

Reader 2: The United States did not join World War II for many years. The country did not want to involve itself in a war that it had no business being in.

Reader 3: Japan decided to make it the Untied States's business.

Reader 2: Japan attacked Pearl Harbor on December 7, 1941. Pearl Harbor is in Hawaii and where many of the U.S. battleships were kept. More than 2,400 lives were lost.

Reader 1: It must have been a horrible time.

Reader 3: The loss of lives and ships was devastating to the United States.

Reader 2: The day after Pearl Harbor, President Roosevelt declared war on Japan.

Reader 4: Japan's friends, Germany and Italy, declared war on the United States, and so the United States officially became part of World War II.

World War II *(cont.)*

Reader 1: If the United States declared war on Japan first, then why did they go to Europe first?

Reader 3: The United States joined the Allies in Europe. Germany had invaded and controlled most of Europe at that time.

Reader 2: The United States joined the British to push the Germans back, and helped to remove the Axis Powers from parts of Europe.

Reader 1: That was on D-Day. Allied troops sailed from England across the English Channel and landed on the beaches of Normandy in France.

Reader 4: The general in charge was General Dwight D. Eisenhower.

Reader 2: D-Day was a pivotal point in the war. By April of 1945, the Allies had conquered a large portion of Germany.

Reader 3: Then the United States had to deal with Japan. President Harry Truman had to decide whether to use the atomic bomb.

Reader 1: Did he decide to use it?

Reader 3: Yes, he did. It devastated Japan and ended the war.

Reader 4: Did the soldiers come home right away?

Reader 2: It took time before we made it home, but we made it as soon as we could. I can still remember my wife sitting on the pier, looking as gorgeous as ever.

Reader 1: That's disgusting.

Reader 4: No, it's romantic. Tell us again how you met.

Reader 3: We've had enough stories for today. Let's call it a day—a red, white, and blue day.

Jim Thorpe

Connections

Literature Connection—*Jim Thorpe: Olympic Champion* by Guernsey Van Riper Jr.
This book is a pictography of the great athlete Jim Thorpe, an American Indian known as one of the best all-around athletes in history. He won an Olympic medal and was an outstanding professional football and baseball player.

Content Connections—Language Arts, Biographies
Jim Thorpe introduces the reader to Jim Thorpe. The story of this great athlete will both amaze and astound you.

Objective

Students will summarize and paraphrase information in texts (e.g., include the main idea and significant supporting details of a reading selection).

Vocabulary

1. Introduce the key vocabulary words from the script. Write each word on the board.
2. Describe the meaning of each word and point out its use in the script. Show pictures that represent the meaning of each word if you have them.
3. Once the students are familiar with the vocabulary words and their definitions, instruct them to write an antonym for each vocabulary word. Remind them that an antonym is a word that has the opposite meaning.
4. Have students write a sentence using each of the antonyms and exchange papers with a partner. Ask students to determine which vocabulary word goes with which antonym.
   - **clan**—a tribe or a group of people
   - **discredited**—harmed or destroyed someone's reputation, dishonored someone
   - **destitute**—poor or penniless
   - **portray**—to depict, to describe, to show
   - **amateur**—an unpaid person in his or her field, someone who is not professional
   - **posthumously**—after death

Before the Reader's Theater

1. Read the title of the script. Ask students to make predictions about the selection based on the title. What do students know about Jim Thorpe? Who was he? What did he do? Is he still alive? Why is he considered one of the greatest athletes of all time?
2. Display the Story Map graphic organizer (page 44 or storymap.pdf). Explain to students that they will use the map to record information about Jim Thorpe. Instruct students to determine the setting, characters, and events in the story. Discuss how using a story map can help identify key points and enable students to summarize and paraphrase what has been read.

Jim Thorpe *(cont.)*

Before the Reader's Theater *(cont.)*

3. Read the script aloud, modeling appropriate reading strategies while you read. To help build fluency and comprehension, it is important for students to hear the script read aloud before practicing on their own.

During the Reader's Theater

1. Divide the class into groups of five to read and practice the script.
2. Students need to decide which character they will play and then highlight their parts in the script (Readers 1–5). They should also mark with a star any places where they need to pause while reading.
3. Give students a few minutes to practice reading with expression in their voices. Additionally, students may decide on a few props or materials to use during their reading. They need to use materials that can be easily acquired or assembled in the classroom.
4. After they have finished practicing, have each group perform the reader's theater for the rest of the class. You may also want them to perform for another class.

After the Reader's Theater

1. As a class, complete the Story Map graphic organizer.
2. Have students create a list of interview questions that they would ask Jim Thorpe if they were given the opportunity. What do they want to know? What advice might Jim Thorpe give them?
3. After students have determined their questions, ask them to research more information about Jim Thorpe. How do they think Jim Thorpe might answer these questions? Have the students write a biography for Jim Thorpe, using a question-and-answer format. Remind them to use their interview questions in the biography.

Response Questions

Group Discussion Questions

- Why do you think Jim Thorpe is known as a famous athlete today? What did he accomplish, both personally and professionally?
- Was Jim Thorpe treated fairly? Why or why not?
- Why do you think Jim Thorpe accomplished so much?

Written Response Question

- Are athletes today the same as they were in the past? What qualities make a great athlete today? Is skill all that is needed?

Name ______________________________ Date ____________________

Story Map

Title:
Setting:
Characters:
Conflict:
Events:
Solution:

Jim Thorpe

By Sarah Kartchner Clark

A reader's theater with five parts

Reader 1: To say that Jim Thorpe is a great athlete is a huge understatement.

Reader 2: Jim Thorpe is the greatest athlete of the twentieth century, and some say that he is the greatest athlete of all time.

Reader 3: Even royalty has declared him the greatest.

Reader 4: That's right. King Gustav V of Sweden told Jim Thorpe, "Sir, you are the greatest athlete in the world."

Reader 5: That's quite a compliment! So, who was Jim Thorpe?

Reader 1: Jim Thorpe was born James Francis Thorpe in a one-room cabin in Oklahoma.

Reader 2: He was born on May 28, 1887.

Reader 3: Jim was part French and part Irish, but he was mostly of Sac and Fox Indian heritage.

Reader 4: He was from the Thunder clan.

Reader 5: Jim was born to Hiram and Charlotte Thorpe.

Reader 1: Jim was born a twin, but his twin brother, Charlie, died of pneumonia when they were nine years old.

Reader 2: Jim's Indian name was Wa-Tho-Huk, which means "Bright Path"—the perfect name for Jim. He definitely had a bright future ahead of him.

Reader 4: Jim was an amazing athlete because he competed so well in so many sports.

Jim Thorpe *(cont.)*

Reader 5: Jim began his athletic career in 1907 at Carlisle Indian Industrial School in Carlisle, Pennsylvania.

Reader 4: At Carlisle, Jim competed in many different sports—track and field, football, baseball, lacrosse, and even ballroom dancing.

Reader 5: In 1913, Jim led Carlisle's football team to the National Collegiate Football Championship, scoring 25 touchdowns and 198 points in one season.

Reader 2: Jim participated in the Summer Olympics in Stockholm, Sweden. He represented the United States, even though he didn't become a United States citizen until 1919.

Reader 1: At the Olympic Games, Jim won the gold medal in both the pentathlon and the decathlon events.

Reader 4: He returned home to America with approximately $50,000 worth of trophies. He was honored with a ticker-tape parade on Broadway in New York City.

Reader 2: A month after the Olympic Games, the Amateur Athletic Union filed charges against Thorpe.

Reader 3: They said that he had played summer baseball with the Rocky Mountain Club for money, which discredited his amateur status.

Reader 4: Jim had played for a small amount of money, so he was stripped of his medals and trophies.

Reader 1: From there, Jim played major league baseball for six years.

Reader 5: Jim played baseball with the New York Giants, the Cincinnati Reds, and later with the Boston Braves.

Reader 1: His best season in baseball was his last.

Jim Thorpe *(cont.)*

Reader 4: He batted .327 in 60 games for the Boston Braves.

Reader 3: Jim Thorpe also played professional football and helped the Canton Bulldogs win the World Championships in 1916, 1917, and 1919.

Reader 1: The Bulldogs were one of the four teams that made up the American Professional Football Association (APFA), which later became the National Football League (NFL).

Reader 2: Jim was elected the APFA's first president, but continued to play football and coach for the Canton Bulldogs.

Reader 5: He played professional football for six different teams between 1920 and 1928. When he retired at age 41, Jim had played a total of 52 NFL games.

Reader 2: After retiring from professional sports, Thorpe became an alcoholic and struggled to support his wife and four children.

Reader 3: He found it difficult to work outside of sports and couldn't hold down a job for very long. He worked as a construction worker, a bouncer, and a movie extra, playing an Indian in Western movies.

Reader 4: Jim also briefly joined the Merchant Marine in 1945.

Reader 3: When people discovered that Thorpe was destitute, organizations across the country raised thousands of dollars to help him.

Reader 5: In 1950, Jim Thorpe was voted the greatest athlete of the half century.

Reader 1: Jim lived to see great things in his life, including a feature film made about himself, "Jim Thorpe: All-American."

Jim Thorpe *(cont.)*

Reader 1: Jim died of a heart attack in 1953 at the age of 65, but his memory and legend live on.

Reader 2: He was the only American athlete to excel as an amateur and professional in three major sports—track and field, football, and baseball.

Reader 3: Soon after his death, a town renamed itself Jim Thorpe, Pennsylvannia.

Reader 4: In 1963, Jim Thorpe was inducted into the Pro Football Hall of Fame in Canton, Ohio.

Reader 5: A statue of Jim stands in the rotunda at the Pro Football Hall of Fame.

Reader 1: Jim Thorpe was named first team Walter Camp All American in 1911 and 1912.

Reader 2: He won gold medals in the decathlon and pentathlon in the 1912 Olympics,

Reader 3: played professional baseball in 1920, and

Reader 4: was elected the first president of what became the National Football League.

Reader 5: He was the first great performer of that league, its highest paid player, and both the precursor and prototype of the weapons of modern football.

Abraham Lincoln

Connections

Literature Connection—*Meet Abraham Lincoln* by Barbara Cary

Meet Abraham Lincoln is a warm, easy-to-understand biography of the sixteenth president of the United States. Lincoln was faced with the nation's greatest crisis in the Civil War and was later assassinated.

Content Connections—Language Arts, Biographies

Abraham Lincoln describes Abraham Lincoln as a child, as an adult, and as the president.

Objective

Students will summarize and paraphrase information in texts (e.g., include the main idea and significant supporting details of a reading selection).

Vocabulary

1. Introduce the key vocabulary words from the script. Write each word on the board.
2. Describe the meaning of each word and point out its use in the script. Show pictures that represent the meaning of each word if you have them.
3. Help students deepen their understanding of the vocabulary words by creating charts of related words and pictures. For the word *maturity*, examples of maturity might include *adult*, *experience*, or *wise*. Post these charts in the room for students to reference throughout the lesson.
   - **maturity**—adulthood
   - **seceded**—broke away or separated
   - **avid**—passionate, fervent, or dedicated
   - **legislature**—an organization of elected representatives; the government
   - **emancipation**—freedom or liberation
   - **reconstruction**—rebuilding or restoration

Before the Reader's Theater

1. Read the title of the script. Ask students to make predictions about the selection based on the title. What do students know about Abraham Lincoln? For what is Abraham Lincoln most famous? What do students know about his life before he become president?
2. Display the Cluster Web graphic organizer (page 51 or clusterweb.pdf). Explain to students that they will use this organizer to record information about Abraham Lincoln.

Abraham Lincoln *(cont.)*

Before the Reader's Theater *(cont.)*

3. Read the script aloud, modeling appropriate reading strategies while you read. To help build fluency and comprehension, it is important for students to hear the script read aloud before practicing on their own.

During the Reader's Theater

1. Divide the class into groups of five to read and practice the script.
2. Students need to decide which character they will play and then highlight their parts in the script (Readers 1–5). They should also mark with a star any places where they need to pause while reading.
3. Give students a few minutes to practice reading with expression in their voices. Additionally, students may decide on a few props or materials to use during their reading. They need to use materials that can be easily acquired or assembled in the classroom.
4. After they have finished practicing, have each group perform the reader's theater for the rest of the class. You may also want them to perform for another class.

After the Reader's Theater

1. Have the class complete the Cluster Web graphic organizer independently or with a partner.
2. Have students research more information about Abraham Lincoln using books, encyclopedias, reference materials, and the Internet.
3. Using this information, students will create a brochure about Abraham Lincoln. The brochure should include key points and information about Abraham Lincoln's life. Have the students include a "Did you Know" section in the brochure with fun facts about Abraham Lincoln.

Response Questions

Group Discussion Questions

- What skills or talents did Abraham Lincoln have that helped him become president? Did his background help him make wise decisions as president?
- What is Abraham Lincoln remembered for today? Do you think it is an accurate picture? Why or why not?
- If Lincoln had lived a longer life, what else might he have accomplished?

Written Response Question

- What skills and characteristics do you think the president of the United States should have? Describe the perfect person to be president.

Name ______________________________ Date ____________________

Cluster Web

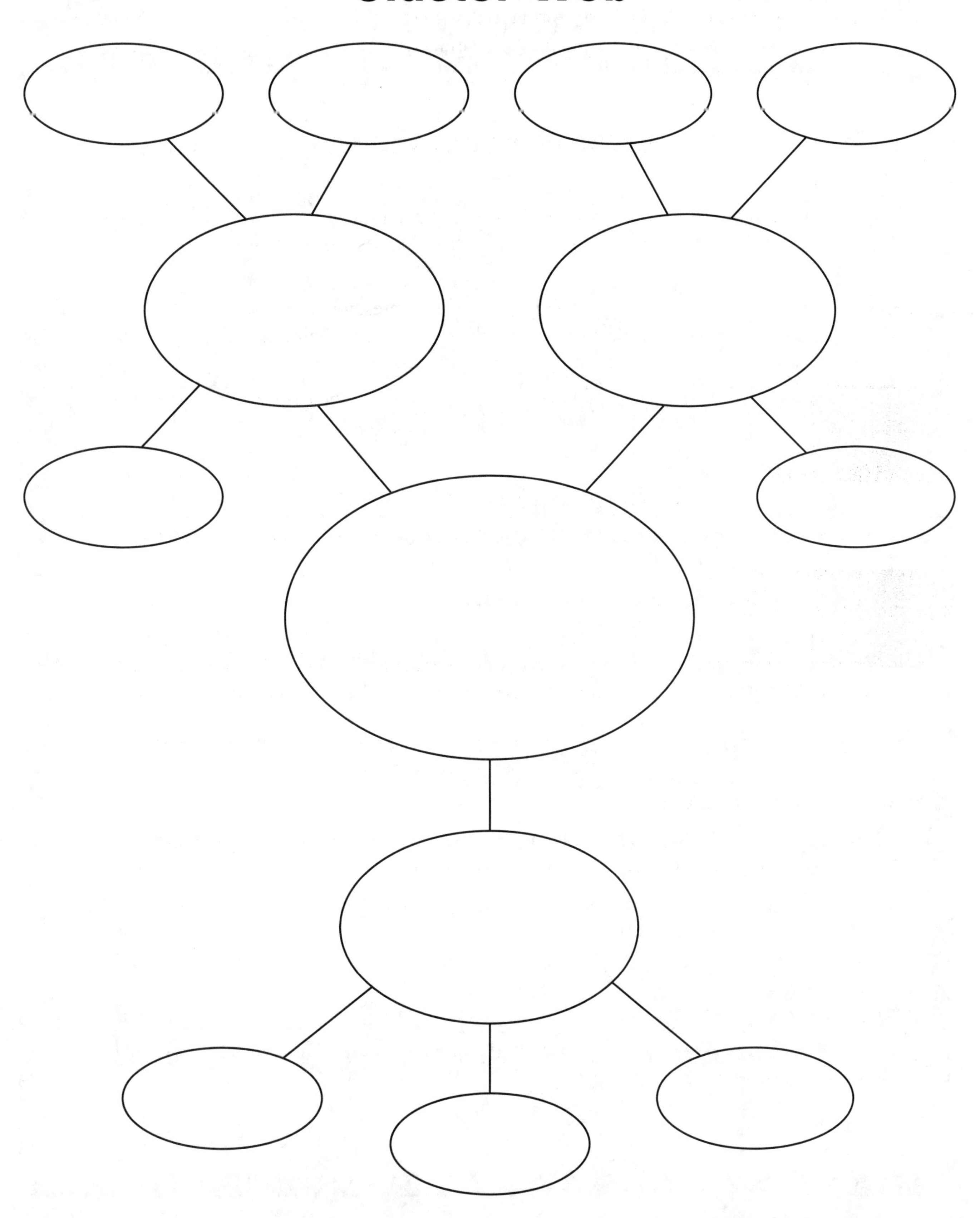

Abraham Lincoln

By Sarah Kartchner Clark

A reader's theater with five parts

Reader 1: What does it take to become president of the United States?

Reader 2: One of our most famous presidents was the most unlikely candidate to be president.

Reader 3: Born on February 12, 1809, Abraham Lincoln was the son of a Kentucky frontiersman.

Reader 4: Abe's family was not rich, and they had to work hard. Abe worked on the family's farm, splitting rails for fences. He also ran the family's store at New Salem, Illinois.

Reader 5: His mother died when he was 10 years old.

Reader 1: Abe's father remarried Sarah Bush Johnston. Abe liked his stepmother very much.

Reader 2: Lincoln was an avid reader, and he got his hands on any book he could.

Reader 3: Later, when the Black Hawk War broke out, Abraham was elected captain in the military.

Reader 4: After the war, Lincoln spent eight years in the Illinois legislature.

Reader 5: In 1839, Lincoln met Mary Todd at a dance. Three years later, he married Mary.

Reader 1: Abraham and Mary had four children—Robert, Edward (Eddie), William (Willie), and Thomas (Tad). All but Tad died at a young age.

Abraham Lincoln *(cont.)*

Reader 2: In 1846, Lincoln ran for the U.S. House of Representatives and won. He was known for his opposition to the Mexican War and slavery.

Reader 3: When he completed his term, he returned home to his law practice. He was more serious about it than ever.

Reader 4: Lincoln's interest in politics surfaced again, and he ran unsuccessfully for the U.S. Senate.

Reader 5: Lincoln opposed the Dred Scott decision in 1857 and gave his famous "House Divided" speech in 1858.

Reader 1: He participated in the famous debates against Stephen A. Douglas.

Reader 4: Lincoln opposed the spread of slavery into the territories, but he wasn't an abolitionist.

Reader 2: Lincoln lost the election to Douglas, but he gained a national reputation.

Reader 3: People were impressed with Lincoln's debating skills. He became the Republican nominee for president.

Reader 4: Lincoln was elected the 16th president of the United States on November 6, 1860. His running mate was Hannibal Hamlin.

Reader 5: The president-elect grew a beard at the suggestion of an 11-year-old girl.

Reader 1: The Lincolns left by train for Washington, D.C., and Lincoln was sworn in on March 4, 1861.

Abraham Lincoln *(cont.)*

Reader 2: Many of the southern states were not happy with the election of Lincoln. As a result, many of these states seceded from the Union.

Reader 3: Lincoln was faced with the greatest crisis of any president. What should he do to keep the United States together?

Reader 4: When the South captured Fort Sumter, Lincoln assembled an army.

Reader 5: He wanted to keep the Union from falling apart. He knew the Union was worth fighting for.

Reader 1: Most people thought the conflict would be short. Instead, the Civil War raged for four years, from 1861 to 1865.

Reader 2: On January 1, 1863, the Emancipation Proclamation was made official.

Reader 3: Lincoln declared freedom for all slaves in the states of the Confederacy that were not under Union control.

Reader 4: In November 1863, Lincoln gave his famous Gettysburg Address in Gettysburg, Pennsylvania.

Reader 5: Lincoln dedicated the Gettysburg battlefield to all the soldiers who had died during the Civil War.

Reader 1: He encouraged all those who were still living to carry on the work of the soldiers who had died.

Reader 2: Ulysses S. Grant was named general-in-chief of the Union armies.

Abraham Lincoln *(cont.)*

Reader 3: The South was exhausted and worn down. In 1864, Lincoln was re-elected president, with Andrew Johnson as his vice president.

Reader 4: Finally, the Civil War ended on April 9, 1865, when General Robert E. Lee surrendered to General Grant.

Reader 5: Two days after the surrender, President Lincoln gave a speech at the White House.

Reader 1: In the speech, he expressed support of allowing African Americans the right to vote.

Reader 2: This upset John Wilkes Booth, who was in the audience. Booth was a Southern sympathizer and a racist.

Reader 4: He hated everything the president was trying to do for African Americans. He was very angry at Lincoln.

Reader 3: On the evening of April 14, 1865, President Lincoln and his wife attended a play at the Ford's Theatre.

Reader 4: During the performance, Booth entered the president's State Box from the rear.

Reader 5: Booth shot President Lincoln in the back of the head.

Reader 1: President Lincoln did not die right away. He was carried to the Petersen House across the street.

Reader 2: Lincoln died the next morning at 7:22 A.M. It was a sad day in America.

Abraham Lincoln *(cont.)*

Reader 3: Lincoln was the first president of the United States to be assassinated. The nation mourned his death and many were stunned by this event.

Reader 4: Lincoln's body was brought to Springfield, Illinois, where he was buried in the Lincoln Tomb in Oak Ridge Cemetery.

Reader 5: Andrew Johnson was sworn in as president and immediately faced the task of reconciling the United States after the devastating Civil War.

Reader 1: After Lincoln's death, President Johnson began the reconstruction of the South.

Reader 4: By the time Congress met in December 1865, most of the reconstruction was complete. Slavery was abolished in many areas.

Reader 2: The nation will always remember President Abraham Lincoln as a man who fought for freedom and the rights of others.

Reader 3: He led the nation during a time of great strife. His legacy is one of determination and perseverance.

Madame Marie Curie

Connections

Literature Connection—*Madame Curie: A Biography* by Eve Curie
Madame Marie Curie's youngest daughter wrote this biography about her mother. The story of hard work, dedication, and accomplishments of a little girl born in Warsaw is an inspiration to young women everywhere.

Content Connections—Language Arts, Biographies
Madame Marie Curie introduces readers to renowned scientists Marie and Pierre Curie. This husband-and-wife team made important discoveries in the fields of physics and chemistry. Both received Nobel Prizes, and Marie Curie received two for her work.

Objective

Students will use text organizers (e.g., headings, topic and summary sentences, graphic features, typeface, chapter titles) to determine the main ideas and to locate information in a text.

Vocabulary

1. Introduce the key vocabulary words from the script. Write each word on the board.
2. Describe the meaning of each word and point out its use in the script. Show pictures that represent the meaning of each word if you have them.
3. Restate the definition or explanation of each vocabulary word. As you do, ask students to respond to your statement by saying the vocabulary word. For example, say to students, "not real and imitation." Then students would respond by saying "artificial."
4. Have students write a sentence for each of the vocabulary words.
   - **detrimental**—harmful, damaging
   - **industrial**—regarding manufacturing, businesses, and factories
   - **tuition**—fees a student pays for schooling
   - **magnetism**—an attraction or pull between two objects
   - **thesis**—a dissertation, or an essay on a specific topic
   - **artificial**—man-made, non-natural, or fake

Before the Reader's Theater

1. Read the title of the script. Ask students to make predictions about the selection based on the title. Ask students what they know about Madame Marie Curie. Who was she? What did she accomplish? What is she known for?
2. Display the Outline Form graphic organizer (page 59 or outlineform.pdf). Explain to students that they will be using this organizer to record information about Madame Marie Curie.

Madame Marie Curie *(cont.)*

Before the Reader's Theater *(cont.)*

3. Read the script aloud, modeling appropriate reading strategies while you read. To help build fluency and comprehension, it is important for students to hear the script read aloud before practicing on their own.

During the Reader's Theater

1. Divide the class into groups of five to read and practice the script.
2. Students need to decide which character they will play and then highlight their parts in the script (Readers 1–5). They should also mark with a star any places where they need to pause while reading.
3. Give students a few minutes to practice reading with expression in their voices. Additionally, students may decide on a few props or materials to use during their reading. They need to use materials that can be easily acquired or assembled in the classroom.
4. After they have finished practicing, have each group perform the reader's theater for the rest of the class. You may also want them to perform for another class.

After the Reader's Theater

1. Have students complete the Outline Form graphic organizer with with a partner.
2. Using the information gained after reading and performing the reader's theater, students will write a newspaper article about the life of Marie Curie. Students can use the Outline Form graphic organizer to assist them with this assignment. Remind them to answer the Who, What, When, Why, Where, and How questions in the newspaper article. If desired, publish a newspaper with all the newspaper articles.

Response Questions

Group Discussion Questions

- Marie worked as a team with her husband, Pierre, at the beginning. How does working as a team make things easier to accomplish? Do you like working as a team?
- Marie paid the ultimate sacrifice for her research and study. How was her life dedicated to mankind?

Written Response Questions

- Marie was the first woman to receive her doctorate degree in physics. What impact did this have on women in her time period and women in the future? What have women accomplished since Marie's time?

Name ______________________________ Date ____________________

Outline Form

Title: ____

I. ____

A. ____

1. ____

2. ____

3. ____

B. ____

1. ____

2. ____

II. ____

A. ____

1. ____

2. ____

B. ____

1. ____

2. ____

3. ____

Conclusion: ____

____

Madame Marie Curie

By Sarah Kartchner Clark

A reader's theater with five parts

Reader 1: Maria Sklodowska, otherwise known as Madame Marie Curie, was born on November 7, 1867, in Warsaw, Poland.

Reader 2: Her family and friends nicknamed her Manya.

Reader 3: Maria's parents raised their children to be patriotic to the country of Poland, but patriotism proved to be harmful to the family.

Reader 4: By 1815, Russia controlled Poland. Maria's father was forced out of a good teaching position because of his beliefs and dedication to the family.

Reader 5: The family suffered great financial difficulties when he lost his job.

Reader 1: Because Maria's parents were teachers, they taught their five children themselves and taught the children to value education.

Reader 2: Before Maria was 11, her eldest sister died of typhus and her mother died of tuberculosis.

Reader 3: Despite these tragedies, Maria graduated from high school at the age of 15 with the highest honors.

Reader 4: Maria began to suffer from a nervous illness. Today, doctors would probably call it depression. She was very tired and did not feel like doing anything.

Reader 5: Maria's father sent her to the countryside to live with a cousin and to spend the year without any responsibilities or concerns in hopes that she would feel better.

Madame Marie Curie *(cont.)*

Reader 1: After recuperating for a year in the country, Maria returned to Warsaw. At this time, women were not permitted to study at the University of Warsaw.

Reader 2: So Maria and her older sister Bronya joined a "floating university." Classes for the floating university were held at night so female students could avoid being caught by the Russian authorities.

Reader 3: Maria and her sister knew that to get a formal education, they would need to attend a university in Western Europe.

Reader 4: The two sisters made a pact. Maria would work as a governess to raise money for Bronya to attend the university.

Reader 1: When Bronya finished school, Bronya would work to raise money for Maria to attend school.

Reader 5: Bronya studied medicine. The owner of a beet sugar factory hired Maria to teach his children. Maria also taught some of the Polish peasant workers how to read.

Reader 4: If the Russian authorities found out she was teaching peasants to read, she would be punished.

Reader 1: Maria used her spare time to read and study. She found that she was good at physics, math, and chemistry.

Reader 2: The Russians didn't allow the Poles to learn laboratory science, but a chemist in the beet sugar factory gave Maria some lessons.

Reader 3: By 1889, Maria's father was earning a good living as the head of a reform school. Maria returned to Warsaw.

Reader 5: For two more years, Maria continued working to send money to Bronya and to raise money for her own schooling.

Madame Marie Curie *(cont.)*

Reader 4: During the evenings and on Sundays, she studied in secret at an illegal lab that trained Polish scientists. This lab was called the "museum."

Reader 5: At 24, Maria had earned enough money to go to the university.

Reader 3: She said farewell to her father and promised to return to Poland one day.

Reader 1: Maria had barely enough money to cover tuition, rent, and a little bit of food.

Reader 4: She also changed her name to Marie from Maria, which was the French version of her name.

Reader 2: Marie was not as well prepared as her fellow students, but she worked and studied very hard to make up the difference.

Reader 3: In just three years, she managed to get a master's degree in math and physics.

Reader 4: She focused so hard on her studies that at times she forgot to eat.

Reader 5: Marie's hard work paid off. She received a scholarship and a job.

Reader 3: The Society for the Encouragement of National Industry hired her to research the magnetic properties of steel.

Reader 1: To do this, Marie needed a laboratory.

Reader 2: The Laboratory Chief at the Paris Municipal School of Industrial Physics and Chemistry was named Pierre Curie. His lab was not one of the best, but he allowed Marie to work there.

Madame Marie Curie *(cont.)*

Reader 1: Pierre was ten years older than Marie and had already made some important scientific discoveries on magnetism and crystals. But he had not done the work necessary to complete a doctoral thesis.

Reader 4: A relationship between Pierre and Marie was blossoming.

Reader 2: Pierre convinced Marie to stay in Paris to continue her studies in science, and Marie convinced Pierre to finish the necessary research to earn his doctoral degree.

Reader 5: Pierre and Marie were married in July of 1895. Marie finished her research on the magnetism of steel.

Reader 4: Two years later, they had their first daughter, Irene.

Reader 3: Pierre's father, a retired doctor, moved in to help care for Irene. Marie and Pierre had a second daughter, Eve.

Reader 1: Marie began searching for a subject in which she could earn her doctoral degree in science.

Reader 5: No woman had ever received such a degree before.

Reader 2: Marie decided to study uranium rays. She was intrigued by what she discovered.

Reader 3: Marie and Pierre began to research radioactive substances. Together, they discovered two radioactive elements: radium and polonium.

Reader 4: In 1903, the Curies won the Nobel Prize for Physics as a result of this discovery.

Reader 5: They shared this award with another physicist, Henri Bacquerel, from France.

Madame Marie Curie *(cont.)*

Reader 1: Three years later, Pierre was run over by a horse drawn carriage and killed instantly. He had been ill for some time and was weak from exposure to radiation over long periods of time.

Reader 2: Less than a month after the funeral, Marie resumed her work and was named the first woman professor at the Sorbonne.

Reader 3: After years of more study, Madame Marie Curie won the 1911 Nobel Prize in chemistry for isolating radium and identifying its chemical properties.

Reader 4: When World War I broke out, Marie thought x-rays, using the radium, would help doctors locate bullets.

Reader 5: She invented x-ray vans and trained 150 female attendants.

Reader 1: On July 4, 1934, Madame Curie died at the age of 67 from leukemia, a disease thought to have been acquired through exposure to high levels of radiation.

Reader 2: Marie did not live to see her daughter, Irene, and her son-in-law, Frederic Joliot-Curie, receive the Nobel Prize for the discovery of artificial radioactivity.

Reader 3: After her death, the Radium Institute was renamed the Curie Institute in Marie's honor.

Reader 4: Marie dedicated her life to science.

Reader 5: Her discoveries set the groundwork for many other new discoveries in the future.

Reader 1: Her dedication, commitment, and hard work are an example to students everywhere!

Harriet Tubman

Connections

Literature Connection—*Harriet Tubman: Conductor on the Underground Railroad* by Ann Petry
An inspiring story of Harriet Tubman's life, this book details the courage and determination that she showed in running away and escaping from slavery. Being free was not enough for Harriet. She wanted to help others. Harriet personally helped liberate hundreds of slaves at the risk of being caught or killed herself.

Content Connections—Language Arts, Biographies
Harriet Tubman introduces the reader to Harriet Tubman, who was born a slave and became known as "Moses," the liberator of many.

Objective

Students will understand similarities and differences within and among literary works from various genres and cultures (e.g., in terms of settings, character types, events, points of view, roles of natural phenomena).

Vocabulary

1. Introduce the key vocabulary words from the script. Write each word on the board.
2. Describe the meaning of each word and point out its use in the script. Show pictures that represent the meaning of each word if you have them.
3. Have students work with a partner to list all the endings that each vocabulary word can have. For example, some of the common endings are *-ing*, *-ed*, *-er*, *-s,* and *-es*. Do these endings change the meaning of the word?
4. Instruct students to write a sentence for each of the vocabulary words using a different ending. For example, students can write a sentence for the word *liberated* instead of *liberator*.
   - **liberator**—a rescuer or redeemer
   - **abolish**—to put an end to, to eliminate
   - **narcolepsy**—a serious sleep disorder
   - **overseer**—a supervisor or manager
   - **pension**—a retirement fund or income

Before the Reader's Theater

1. Read the title of the script. Ask students to make predictions about the selection based on the title. What do students know about Harriet Tubman? What type of information do they predict they will learn about her?
2. Display the Compare and Contrast graphic organizer (page 67 or compareandcontrast.pdf). Tell students they will use this to organizer to record information about Harriet Tubman and Abraham Lincoln.

Harriet Tubman *(cont.)*

Before the Reader's Theater *(cont.)*

3. Read the script aloud, modeling appropriate reading strategies while you read. To help build fluency and comprehension, it is important for students to hear the script read aloud before practicing on their own.

During the Reader's Theater

1. Divide the class into groups of five to read and practice the script.
2. Students need to decide which character they will play and then highlight their parts in the script (Readers 1–5). They should also mark with a star any places where they need to pause while reading.
3. Give students a few minutes to practice reading with expression in their voices. Additionally, students may decide on a few props or materials to use during their reading. They need to use materials that can be easily acquired or assembled in the classroom.
4. After they have finished practicing, have each group perform the reader's theater for the rest of the class. You may also want them to perform for another class.

After the Reader's Theater

1. Have students complete the Compare and Contrast graphic organizer independently, in pairs, or in small groups.
2. Ask students to research more information about Harriet Tubman using books, encyclopedias, reference materials, and the Internet.
3. With this information, the students will create a time line of Harriet Tubman's life. Students will write a brief summary of each major event in her life. Pictures and drawings should be used to illustrate the time line.

Response Questions

Group Discussion Questions

- Harriet Tubman was an inspiring person. How do you think she was able to accomplish so much in her life?
- Do you think Harriet's background helped her to be such a daring and noble person? How? What is your background helping you to become?

Written Response Question

- Can you think of another person in history who was willing to sacrifice so much for something or someone? Describe this person and list his or her similarities to Harriet Tubman.

Name ______________________________ Date ____________________

Compare and Contrast

How are these two alike?

How are these two different?

Harriet Tubman

By Sarah Kartchner Clark

A reader's theater with five parts

Reader 1: Have you ever met anyone who would be willing to risk his or her life for the freedom of others?

Reader 2: Harriet Tubman is one of those people. She stands out in history as an example of courage, bravery,and determination.

Reader 3: Harriet was born a slave in 1819 or 1820 in Dorchester, Maryland. She was of pure African ancestry. She was named Harriet Ross after her two parents.

Reader 4: Harriet's childhood was difficult. She was whipped, even as a young child, by her cruel and harsh slave owners.

Reader 5: At 12 years old, she was injured seriously when she was hit very hard in the head. An overseer beat her for not helping him tie up a slave who had tried to escape.

Reader 4: It was said that she suffered from narcolepsy as a result of this injury.

Reader 1: Harriet married a man by the name of John Tubman. John was a free African American.

Reader 2: Harriet worried that she would be sold further south by her owners, so after five years, she decided to try to escape.

Reader 5: John opposed her plans to flee north, so Harriet decided to go alone.

Reader 3: A white neighbor gave Harriet a piece of paper that had two names on it and told her how to find the first house on her path to freedom.

Harriet Tubman *(cont.)*

Reader 4: When Harriet got to the first house, the owners quickly put her inside a wagon and covered her with a sack. They took her to the next house.

Reader 5: She continued her escape in this manner, traveling from house to house, until she arrived in Pennsylvania.

Reader 1: Once she had her freedom, Harriet wanted to help others.

Reader 2: In Philadelphia, Harriet met a man named William Still.

Reader 5: Still was the Philly Stationmaster of the Underground Railroad.

Reader 3: This wasn't a regular railroad that ran underground. This railroad was very different.

Reader 4: For many of the slaves who lived in the slave states before and during the Civil War, the Underground Railroad was the only way to freedom.

Reader 5: No one knows exactly when it started, but history documents slaves escaping as early as the 1700s.

Reader 1: The Underground Railroad was a network of paths through river crossings, woods, fields, wagons, boats, ships, and trains.

Reader 2: The name probably came from the popularity of the new railroads in America.

Reader 3: The Underground Railroad was "conducted" by brave men and women who were willing to risk their lives to help escort the slaves to freedom.

Reader 4: Many of these people were called abolitionists. They wanted to abolish slavery.

Harriet Tubman *(cont.)*

Reader 3: Runaway slaves usually traveled alone or in small groups. They were always at risk of being caught.

Reader 5: William Still asked Harriet to become part of the Underground Railroad. Harriet agreed and became a "conductor."

Reader 1: Harriet became known as "Moses" because she led her people to freedom just as Moses did. She made more than 19 trips to the South and helped liberate more than 300 slaves.

Reader 2: At one point, a reward of $40,000 was posted for the capture of Harriet Tubman.

Reader 3: In 1851, Harriet began trying to relocate her family members to Canada. Harriet was making a big difference in the lives of others.

Reader 4: Harriet was described as fearless and dedicated to the cause of freedom for slaves. She risked her own life on numerous occasions.

Reader 5: Harriet was an activist who helped John Brown organize the raid at Harper's Ferry. She couldn't go herself because of illness.

Reader 1: It was said that Harriet thought John Brown, rather than Abraham Lincoln, was the great liberator of her people.

Reader 2: When the Civil War started, Harriet worked as a soldier, a spy, and a nurse. She served for a time at Fortress Monroe.

Reader 4: She was particularly helpful to the army because of her knowledge of secret paths and roads as a result of her work with the Underground Railroad.

Harriet Tubman *(cont.)*

Reader 3: When the war was over, she was denied any payment for her wartime service. Can you believe that?

Reader 4: After the Civil War, Harriet returned to Auburn, New York. Her husband John died two years later.

Reader 3: She married Nelson Davis, who was 10 years younger.

Reader 5: Harriet helped the city of Auburn remain active in many causes. One of those causes was the support of women's rights.

Reader 1: She spent her last days in poverty and did not receive a pension of $20 a month until 30 years after the Civil War.

Reader 2: In 1908, she spent this money to build a wooden house that served as her home, as well as a home for the elderly and the poor.

Reader 1: Harriet continued to help and serve others.

Reader 3: It was here that Harriet herself was cared for before she died in 1913. Harriet was buried with military honors in Ft. Hill Cemetery in Auburn.

Reader 4: Harriet received many honors and tributes in her life, including a medal from Queen Victoria.

Reader 3: Her wooden house was later named the Harriet Tubman Home.

Reader 5: Harriet left a legacy of love and protection of the human spirit. She advanced the cause of freedom as well as human rights.

Reader 4: Harriet will live on in the memories of others for many years to come.

Earthquakes

Connections

Literature Connection—*Eyewitness: Volcano & Earthquake* by Susanna Van Rose
This book provides an eyewitness view of what happens during and after an earthquake.

Content Connections—Science, Earthquakes
Earthquakes tells about the history of famous earthquakes and shares information on what to do during an earthquake.

Objective

Students will summarize and paraphrase information in texts (e.g., include the main idea and significant supporting details of a reading selection).

Vocabulary

1. Introduce the key vocabulary words from the script. Write each word on the board.
2. Describe the meaning of each word and point out its use in the script. Show pictures that represent the meaning of each word if you have them.
3. Ask students to help you write a short story, using all six vocabulary words. Write the story on chart paper.
   - **excavate**—to dig out, to unearth
   - **rubble**—debris, ruins, or wreckage
   - **seismic**—earthshaking
   - **crust**—a shell or an outer layer
   - **mantle**—a layer or coating
   - **faults**—an imperfection or a flaw

Before the Reader's Theater

1. Read the title of the script. Ask students to make predictions about the selection based on the title and share any information they know about earthquakes. How do earthquakes happen? Have any students ever been in an earthquake? What did they do?
2. Display the Topic Diagram graphic organizer (page 74 or topicdiagram.pdf). Tell students they will use this organizer to record information about earthquakes.

Earthquakes *(cont.)*

Before the Reader's Theater *(cont.)*

3. Read the script aloud, modeling appropriate reading strategies while you read. To help build fluency and comprehension, it is important for students to hear the script read aloud before practicing on their own.

During the Reader's Theater

1. Divide the class into groups of four to read and practice the script.
2. Students need to decide which character they will play and then highlight their parts in the script (Readers 1–4). They should also mark with a star any places where they need to pause while reading.
3. Give students a few minutes to practice reading with expression in their voices. Additionally, students may decide on a few props or materials to use during their reading. They need to use materials that can be easily acquired or assembled in the classroom.
4. After they have finished practicing, have each group perform the reader's theater for the rest of the class. You may also want them to perform for another class.

After the Reader's Theater

1. As a class, complete the Topic Diagram graphic organizer.
2. Have students research more information about earthquakes using books, encyclopedias, reference materials, and the Internet.
3. Using this information, students will create a brochure about earthquakes, containing key points and information about how earthquakes happen and how to be prepared in case of an earthquake.

Response Questions

Group Discussion Questions

- Have you ever been in an earthquake? What happened? What did you do? What happened to the city in which you lived?
- Which natural disaster are you most afraid of and why?

Written Response Question

- How do you think we can best prepare for an earthquake? What responsibility does the government have in helping people prepare for and recover from an earthquake? Explain your answer.

Name ______________________________ Date ______________________

Topic Diagram

Topic

Subheading

Event/Concept 1	Event/Concept 2	Event/Concept 3

Subheading

Event/Concept 4	Event/Concept 5	Event/Concept 6

Conclusions

Additional Information

Earthquakes

By Sarah Kartchner Clark

A reader's theater with four parts

All: Beep! Beep! Beep! Beep!

Reader 1: This just in! An earthquake has just occurred in California!

Reader 2: That's right. Officials say that many people survived, but help is needed to excavate others buried by the rubble.

Reader 3: Rescue workers are on the scene now. Back to you in the studio.

Reader 4: Thanks. Can you tell us how earthquakes happen? Is someone at fault? Is this something that could have been prevented?

Reader 1: Earthquakes are a natural disaster. People do not cause earthquakes.

Reader 3: The outer layer of Earth, otherwise known as the crust, consists of several pieces called plates.

Reader 2: The plates under the ocean are called oceanic plates, and others are called continental plates.

Reader 1: The plates move around Earth's mantle, which lies under the crust.

Reader 4: Are the moving plates the cause of earthquakes?

Reader 1: Yes. The plates move continuously, bump into one another, brush past one another, or even pull away from one another.

Reader 2: Earthquakes occur when two plates brush up against each other or move over each other.

Earthquakes *(cont.)*

Reader 4: How fast do these plates move?

Reader 3: It has been said that Earth's plates move as slowly as fingernails growing.

All: Beep! Beep! Beep! Beep!

Reader 1: Word is in that there are more survivors than originally thought.

Reader 2: We mentioned that earthquakes also happen far from the edges of Earth's plates. Earthquakes can also happen along faults.

Reader 3: Faults are cracks in Earth's crust where the plates have pulled apart.

Reader 1: Earthquakes usually happen when the rock underground suddenly breaks along a fault line. Back to you in the studio.

Reader 4: Thanks. What is happening now? Reports have been filed here saying that the government has increased the number of aid stations that are available.

Reader 2: That information seems to be correct. The landscape is a mess. Everything has been turned upside down. People need a place to go.

Reader 3: This earthquake definitely caught people by surprise.

Reader 4: Why is that?

Reader 3: One reason is that the scientists thought the next earthquake would be closer to the San Andreas fault line.

Reader 1: They didn't expect it to be this far south of that fault.

Earthquakes *(cont.)*

Reader 4: So what causes the earth to shake?

Reader 2: The sudden release of energy causes seismic waves that shake the ground.

Reader 1: When two blocks of rock or two plates rub against each other, they sometimes stick.

Reader 2: They don't slide smoothly. They catch on each other.

Reader 1: But the rocks continue pushing against each other. The pressure builds and causes the rocks to break, creating the earthquake.

All: Beep! Beep! Beep! Beep!

Reader 3: This report is coming to you live from California.

Reader 2: Yes. Apparently this earthquake was a 6.5 on the Richter scale.

Reader 1: That's a very intense earthquake.

Reader 4: Exactly what is the Richter scale?

Reader 3: The Richter Scale rates the power, or magnitude, of the earthquake. The higher the number, the more intense the earthquake.

Reader 2: Records show that the Richter Scale has registered a 9.5 earthquake, although even greater earthquakes have occurred in the earth's history.

All: Beep! Beep! Beep! Beep!

Reader 4: We have just gotten word that many smaller earthquakes have happened. Are you experiencing any of these?

Earthquakes *(cont.)*

Reader 1: We are standing on ground where shopping centers, banks, and strip malls were once located. The ground has been destroyed. Very little remains of the landscape except wreckage, cracks, and crevices.

Reader 2: Indeed, many smaller quakes are happening, but an earthquake that rates lower than a 4.0 on the Richter scale does little damage.

Reader 4: How can people prepare for earthquakes?

Reader 3: Scientific research has increased our knowledge of earthquakes in the last 50 years.

Reader 1: As a result, many changes have happened in the field of construction engineering.

Reader 3: The way we construct buildings has changed to accommodate earthquakes. Buildings are built to absorb the shock of earthquakes.

Reader 4: What should a person do in an earthquake?

Reader 2: If caught in an earthquake at home, hide under a sturdy desk or table, or stand in an interior doorway.

Reader 3: Avoid windows that may shatter, or bookshelves and furniture that could fall on you.

Reader 1: Know how to turn off the utilities. More accidents can happen because of leaks and cracks in the water heater or in gas or electricity lines. Above all, stay calm! Back to you.

Reader 4: There you have it, ladies and gentlemen. The latest details on the earthquake in California. Let's hope that all survivors are found quickly and can return home.

Space Exploration

Connections

Literature Connection—*A History of Space Exploration* by Tim Furniss
This book recounts the history of space exploration, beginning with the first liquid-propelled rocket in 1926. It also discusses future missions that are currently in the planning stage.

Content Connections—Science, Astronomy
Space Exploration explains the qualifications for the first astronauts and the evolution of space travel.

Objective

Students will summarize and paraphrase information in texts (e.g., include the main idea and significant supporting details of a reading selection).

Vocabulary

1. Introduce the key vocabulary words from the script. Write each word on the board.
2. Describe the meaning of each word and point out its use in the script. Show pictures that represent the meaning of each word if you have them.
3. Help students deepen their understanding of the vocabulary words by creating a chart of related words. For the word *critical*, examples might include *important*, *crucial*, *key*, and *necessary*. Post these charts in the room for students to refer to throughout the lesson.
   - **credited**—recognized for, attributed to
   - **critical**—serious or severe
   - **launching**—initiating or introducing
   - **psychological**—mental or emotional
   - **eliminated**—gotten rid of or done away with

Before the Reader's Theater

1. Read the title of the script. Ask students to make predictions about the selection based on the title. What will this script be about? Is it fiction or nonfiction? Why do they think so? Ask the class to share knowledge about space exploration. What are the names of some astronauts?
2. Display the Comprehension Chart graphic organizer (page 81 or comprehensionchart.pdf). Tell students they will use the organizer to record information about space exploration.

Space Exploration *(cont.)*

Before the Reader's Theater *(cont.)*

3. Read the script aloud, modeling appropriate reading strategies while you read. To help build fluency and comprehension, it is important for students to hear the script read aloud before practicing on their own.

During the Reader's Theater

1. Divide the class into groups of five to read and practice the script.
2. Students need to decide which character they will play and then highlight their parts in the script (Readers 1–5). They should also mark with a star any places where they need to pause while reading.
3. Give students a few minutes to practice reading with expression in their voices. Additionally, students may decide on a few props or materials to use during their reading. They need to use materials that can be easily acquired or assembled in the classroom.
4. After they have finished practicing, have each group perform the reader's theater for the rest of the class. You may also want them to perform for another class.

After the Reader's Theater

1. As a class, complete the Comprehension Chart graphic organizer.
2. Ask students to research more information about space travel and astronauts. Students can conduct research on the Internet to find out information about past space exploration as well as future plans.
3. Using this information, students will create a time line of space travel on poster paper that has ample space for a time line. Instruct students to use pictures and diagrams to illustrate the posters.

Response Questions

Group Discussion Questions

- What do you think the qualifications are to be an astronaut today? What type of person do you think is suitable to travel in outer space?
- Do you think there should be a space program for children to be astronauts? Why or why not? Give some reasons why such a program would be beneficial. State reasons why children should not travel into space.

Written Response Question

- Have you ever dreamed of traveling into space? Write a resume to NASA explaining why you would make the perfect astronaut. Be sure to list your goals and reasons for going into space.

Name ______________________________ Date ______________________

Comprehension Chart

Topic

Title:

Who is the audience?

Thesis Statement:

Supporting statements/examples from text:

Supporting statements/examples from text:

Supporting statements/examples from text:

Conclusion:

Space Exploration

By Sarah Kartchner Clark

A reader's theater with five parts

Reader 1: Have you ever dreamed of flying into space? People have been dreaming of space travel since the beginning of time.

Reader 2: Aviation history officially began on December 17, 1903, at Kill Devil Hill near Kitty Hawk, North Carolina.

Reader 3: Orville Wright, by the flip of a coin, was the first man to take a powered, sustained, and controlled flight.

Reader 4: He flew 120 feet in 12 seconds, and that accomplishment placed him in the history books. Flight and space travel have continued to advance since the first flight.

Reader 5: Robert Goddard played a role in rocketry that took the United States to the next level. Today he is considered the most important figure in American rocket history.

Reader 1: Hermann Oberth in Germany and Kanstantin Tsiolkovsky in Russia also contributed to the science of rocketry.

Reader 2: These three men are called the "Fathers of Modern Rocketry."

Reader 3: Robert Goddard is credited with launching the first liquid-powered rocket on March 16, 1926.

Reader 4: Before Goddard's rocket, rockets were based on solid fuel or gunpowder.

Reader 1: Goddard's liquid-fueled rocket was a critical advance in rocket science.

Reader 5: Rockets didn't have the power necessary to fly to the moon.

Space Exploration *(cont.)*

Reader 1: Goddard's experiments inspired another aviation pioneer named Charles Lindbergh.

Reader 3: In 1927, Lindbergh became the first person to cross the Atlantic Ocean in a nonstop flight.

Reader 2: Progress in aviation and rocketry continued throughout World War I and World War II.

Reader 4: Dropping bombs and using other weapons in flight was a new concept at the time.

Reader 3: By the end of World War II, Edwards Air Force Base (known as Muroc at this time) was the place to be if you were a pilot. Planes were able to reach Mach .80.

Reader 2: Up to this point, the sound barrier had not yet been broken. But that would soon change.

Reader 5: Even though Captain Chuck Yeager was a junior pilot at the time, he was certainly the best pilot.

Reader 4: He was a World War II ace. He believed that the sound barrier could indeed be broken.

Reader 1: On Yeager's first attempt to break the sound barrier, he reached .997, the closest anyone had ever come to breaking the sound barrier.

Reader 2: Then, that weekend, Yeager broke two ribs riding a horse.

Reader 4: He didn't want to miss the chance to break this record so he had a doctor tape his ribs and he didn't tell anyone else about the injury.

Reader 3: So on October 14, 1947, Yeager became the first person to finally break the sound barrier.

Space Exploration *(cont.)*

Reader 4: The government kept this information secret, so Yeager didn't get a ticker-tape parade like Charles Lindbergh did.

Reader 5: After World War II, the cloud of the Cold War hung over the United States. The space race was on.

Reader 1: The United States was coming closer and closer to sending a man into space, but had not succeeded.

Reader 2: On October 4, 1957, the USSR surprised the United States and shocked the world by launching Sputnik I into space.

Reader 3: Sputnik was the first man-made earth-orbiting satellite. This gave the USSR a huge political advantage.

Reader 4: Sputnik circled Earth every 90 minutes. Its beeping radio signal was a constant reminder that the United States was behind in the space race.

Reader 5: Sputnik II wasn't far behind. In November of 1957, Laika, a dog, became the first living organism launched into space on Sputnik II.

Reader 1: Laika died because her oxygen supply ran out.

Reader 4: However, the scientific data that was collected on the effects of weightlessness and space travel on a living animal was very helpful to future rocket science and space travel.

Reader 2: In January of 1958, Explorer I, the first U.S. satellite, was launched.

Reader 5: The United States had a long way to go to catch up with the USSR in the space race.

Reader 3: Scientists began to think about sending a man into space.

Space Exploration *(cont.)*

Reader 2: But it didn't happen overnight.

Reader 3: In the year 1959, the National Aeronautics and Space Administration, also known as NASA, began a search for pilots who would participate in the new manned space flight program.

Reader 4: Competition was heating up against the Russians, and the United States wanted to be the first country to put a man into space.

Reader 5: The requirements to be an astronaut were very specific. Not just anyone could apply for the job of astronaut.

Reader 1: Anyone applying to be an astronaut could be no taller than 5 feet 11 inches tall...

Reader 2: Had to be younger than 40 years old...

Reader 3: Had to be in excellent physical condition...

Reader 4: And had to have a bachelor's degree in engineering.

Reader 5: But that wasn't all. An astronaut also needed to be a certified jet pilot, a graduate of test pilot school, and have at least 1,500 hours of flying time.

Reader 3: NASA asked the United States military to submit names of people who met these qualifications.

Reader 4: More that 500 men qualified.

Reader 1: Their military and medical records were examined, and they were given psychological as well as technical tests.

Reader 5: Candidates also participated in personal interviews. Some candidates were eliminated and some decided that they didn't want to participate.

Space Exploration *(cont.)*

Reader 1: In April of 1959, NASA announced the selection of seven men…the first American astronauts.

Reader 2: These men were M. Scott Carpenter, L. Gordon Cooper Jr., Virgil I. "Gus" Grissom, Donald K. "Deke" Slayton, John H. Glenn Jr., Walter M. Schirra Jr., and Alan B. Shepard Jr.

Reader 3: Do you recognize any of these names?

Reader 4: Some of these men accomplished great things at NASA and are parts of legends and stories that will be told for many years to come.

Reader 5: In the following years, NASA identified more astronauts and brought them onboard. Spacecraft were built to accelerate to great speeds.

Reader 1: Steps were taken to ensure the safety of the astronauts onboard the rocket.

Reader 2: In 1961, President John F. Kennedy challenged NASA to put a man on the moon and to bring him safely back to Earth.

Reader 3: Finally, on July 20, 1969, Neil Armstrong became the first man to take steps on the moon.

Reader 4: His famous words, "That's one small step for man, one giant leap for mankind" were heard throughout the world.

Reader 5: Mankind had finally done it!

Reader 1: The United States, along with other countries throughout the world, has worked to improve understanding of outer space.

Reader 2: We hope that what is learned will make life better here on Earth, as well as allow more people to travel in space.

Reader 3: To infinity and beyond…

Plant Life

Connections

Literature Connection—*How a Plant Grows* by Bobbie Kalman
This book includes full-color illustrations showing each stage as a seed grows into a plant. The book also explains the importance of plants in the food chain and how different types of plants grow.

Content Connections—Science, Biology
Plant Life explains how seeds germinate and grow. Students will learn the importance of plant life and how plants beautify and decorate the world.

Objective

Students will summarize and paraphrase information in texts (e.g., include the main idea and significant supporting details of a reading selection).

Vocabulary

1. Introduce the key vocabulary words from the script. Write each word on the board.
2. Describe the meaning of each word and point out its use in the script. Show pictures that represent the meaning of each word if you have them.
3. Help students create meaningful sample sentences with the vocabulary words. Provide a sentence starter for students to use for the first word. Write the sentence starter on the board and read it aloud. Then have students work in pairs to complete the sentence. Repeat this activity for the other vocabulary words.
   - **germinate**—sprouts, grows, or develops
   - **reproduce**—duplicate or repeat
   - **emerge**—come out or materialize
   - **immature**—small or not fully formed
   - **temporary**—momentary or brief
   - **edible**—safe to eat; not poisonous

Before the Reader's Theater

1. Read the title of the script. Ask students to make predictions about the selection based on the title. Do the students know how a seed germinates? What does a plant need to grow? Are all plants the same? How do you know how much water each plant should get?
2. Display the Idea Web graphic organizer (page 89 or ideaweb.pdf). Tell students that they will use the organizer to record information about plant life.

Plant Life *(cont.)*

Before the Reader's Theater *(cont.)*

3. Read the script aloud, modeling appropriate reading strategies while you read. To help build fluency and comprehension, it is important for students to hear the script read aloud before practicing on their own.

During the Reader's Theater

1. Divide the class into groups of four to read and practice the script.
2. Students need to decide which character they will play and then highlight their parts in the script (Readers 1–4). They should also mark with a star any places where they need to pause while reading.
3. Give students a few minutes to practice reading with expression in their voices. Additionally, students may decide on a few props or materials to use during their reading. They need to use materials that can be easily acquired or assembled in the classroom.
4. After they have finished practicing, have each group perform the reader's theater for the rest of the class. You may also want them to perform for another class.

After the Reader's Theater

1. Have students complete the Idea Web graphic organizer independently or with a partner.
2. Have students research more information about plant life and how seeds grow, using books, encyclopedias, reference materials, and the Internet.
3. Using this information, students will write a report on their findings. Remind them to paraphrase words rather than copy the information they find. Instruct the students to list the sources in a bibliography.

Response Questions

Group Discussion Questions

- Have you ever planted a seed? Did it grow? Tell us about your experience.
- What are the main things that a plant needs to survive?
- What role does plant life have in the food chain?

Written Response Question

- What type of garden would you grow? What plants would you include and why? Where would you plant your garden? What tips and techniques do you plan to follow?

Name ______________________ Date ______________

Idea Web

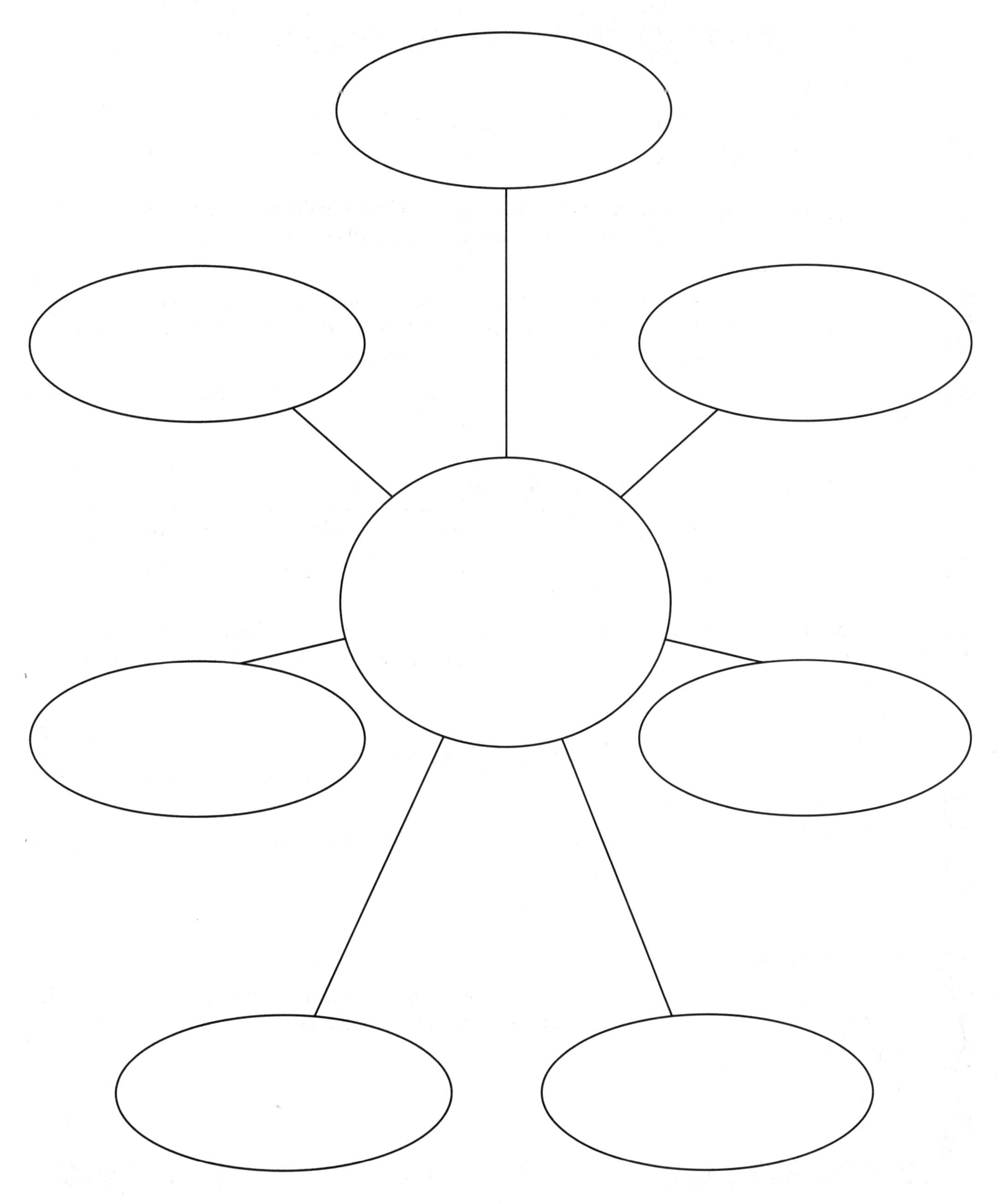

Plant Life

By Sarah Kartchner Clark

A reader's theater with four parts

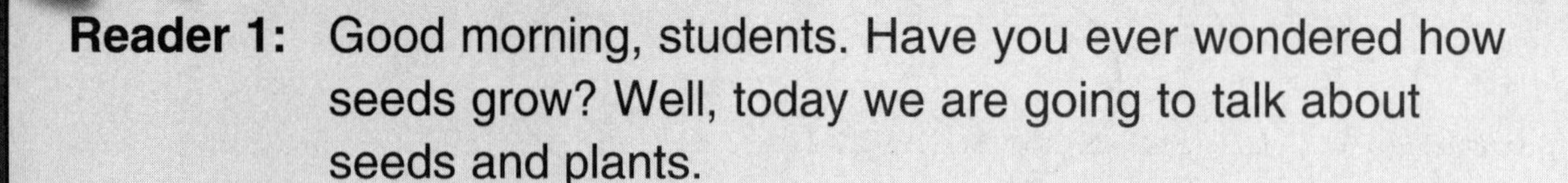

Reader 1: Good morning, students. Have you ever wondered how seeds grow? Well, today we are going to talk about seeds and plants.

Reader 2: Exactly what are the seeds in the plants?

Reader 3: Aren't seeds the middle part of the plant?

Reader 1: Well, some seeds are found in the centers of plants, but seeds can also be found in all different places on a plant.

Reader 4: What is a seed?

Reader 1: The seed of a plant allows the plant to make more plants just like itself. Seeds allow the plant to reproduce.

Reader 2: How does this work?

Reader 1: Inside each seed is a tiny, living plant called an embryo.

Reader 3: Wow. That's a big word.

Reader 1: We will learn many big words as we study about plants. But we will take each word one at a time and discuss it.

Reader 4: Sounds good.

Reader 1: An embryo is just a fancy name for the tiny plant living inside each seed. With the right combination of water, oxygen, and temperature, this tiny plant will burst out, emerge from the seed, and begin its life.

Reader 2: What happens if the embryo doesn't get the right combination of water, oxygen, and temperature?

Plant Life *(cont.)*

Reader 1: That's a great question. The seed will stay dormant, or asleep, until the seed germinates.

Reader 3: Do seeds need food to live? I think all living things need food.

Reader 1: Yes, seeds need food to live. Each seed contains a temporary supply of food called the endosperm. The endosperm is packed around the embryo.

Reader 4: What else does a seed have?

Reader 1: All seeds have a seed coat.

Reader 2: A coat? Does a coat help the seed stay dry?

Reader 1: It does sound funny, but a seed coat is very important. It actually protects the embryo inside the seed from damage or from drying out.

Reader 3: So what happens next? This is interesting!

Reader 1: Oh good. Next, an immature root starts to emerge from the seed. The name of this root is the radicle.

Reader 4: That sounds serious.

Reader 1: Radicle is just a fancy name for a baby root.

Reader 2: What comes after the radicle?

Reader 1: The plumule, which contains the stem and the leaves, comes after the radicle. The plumule searches for light and air, so it shoots upwards.

Reader 3: These words sound as if you are speaking a foreign language!

Plant Life *(cont.)*

Reader 1: It is scientific language. When the seed begins growing, the endosperm, or the temporary supply of food, begins forming the seed leaves.

Reader 2: What's the scientific name for that?

Reader 1: The scientific name is cotyledon.

Reader 4: I knew it was going to have a fancy name, too!

Reader 1: The cotyledon provides food for the plant until it can form true leaves.

Reader 2: You mean the plant doesn't start out with leaves?

Reader 1: Oh no. All the parts of the plant take time to grow, as you and I take time to grow.

Reader 3: Do we have a cotyledon?

Reader 1: No, silly, you don't have any leaves.

Reader 4: Keep going. What happens next?

Reader 1: Well, as I said before, all these steps take time. The next step in the process is that the roots, stems, and leaves begin to form. The plant is becoming established. It begins to look like the plants you see in your yard.

Reader 2: What do the roots, stem, and leaves do for the plant?

Reader 1: That's another good question. The roots, stem, and leaves each have an important job.

Reader 3: I know what the stem does. It supports the plant as it grows upward.

Reader 4: Don't the roots help keep the plant supported in the ground?

Plant Life *(cont.)*

Reader 1: You are smart kids. The stem also helps to transport nutrients throughout the plant. The roots also collect water and store nutrients.

Reader 2: The leaves help protect the plant, and they carry nutrients, too.

Reader 1: The plant is now ready to begin producing flowers and a new batch of seeds to complete its life cycle.

Reader 3: So then it starts all over again?

Reader 1: That's right. The process begins all over again.

Reader 4: I have heard that seeds are poisonous.

Reader 1: Some seeds can be poisonous, but many others we eat. Most seeds are not poisonous.

Reader 2: What are some of the seeds we eat?

Reader 4: We eat sunflower seeds.

Reader 3: What else?

Reader 1: We also eat peas and lima beans. These are seeds.

Reader 4: Are humans the only animals that eat seeds?

Reader 1: Oh no. All kinds of animals eat seeds. Birds, mammals, and insects all eat seeds. Plants and seeds are at the bottom of most food chains. Plants are the foundation of most living things. Where would we be without seeds?

Reader 2: I don't know, but I'm hungry. Let's go eat some seeds!

Reader 1: Great job, class. Now where are some edible seeds?

Electricity

Connections

Literature Connection—*Eyewitness: Electricity* by Steve Parker
This book offers a child's perspective of electricity and where it comes from. It details step-by-step instructions on the history of electricity, how electricity is formed, how it works, and how our knowledge has increased through the years.

Content Connections—Science, Electricity
Electricity takes students on a reading field trip about electricity in an easy to read and understand format.

Objective

Students will summarize and paraphrase information in texts (e.g., include the main idea and significant supporting details of a reading selection).

Vocabulary

1. Introduce the key vocabulary words from the script. Write each word on the board. Read each word aloud.
2. Describe the meaning of each word and point out its use in the script. Show pictures that represent the meaning of each word if you have them.
3. Have students work in small groups to create visual representations for the vocabulary words. Cut a sheet of paper into several pieces. Put students into groups, and give each group a piece of chart paper. Assign one word to each group. Then have each group create a visual represntation for its assigned word. Allow time for each group to share their posters with the class.
   - **atom**—an article
   - **electron**—a small particle with a negative charge
   - **electrocuted**—to be killed with electricity
   - **conduct**—to control or run (electricity)
   - **transmit**—to send out, put out
   - **insulator**—filling, or padding that protects against electricity, temperature, or sound

Before the Reader's Theater

1. Read the title of the script. Ask students to make predictions about the selection based on the title. Ask the class to share information about electricity. What is electricity? How does it work? How was it discovered?
2. Display the Picture the Process graphic organizer (page 96 or pictureprocess.pdf). Tell students that they will use this organizer to record information about electricity.

Electricity *(cont.)*

Before the Reader's Theater *(cont.)*

3. Read the script aloud, modeling appropriate reading strategies while you read. To help build fluency and comprehension, it is important for students to hear the script read aloud before practicing on their own.

During the Reader's Theater

1. Divide the class into groups of three to read and practice the script.
2. Students need to decide which character they will play and then highlight their parts in the script (Readers 1–3). They should also mark with a star any places where they need to pause while reading.
3. Give students a few minutes to practice reading with expression in their voices. Additionally, students may decide on a few props or materials to use during their reading. They need to use materials that can be easily acquired or assembled in the classroom.
4. After they have finished practicing, have each group perform the reader's theater for the rest of the class. You may also want them to perform for another class.

After the Reader's Theater

1. As a class, complete the Picture the Process graphic organizer.
2. Have students research more information about electricity, using books, encyclopedias, reference materials, and the Internet. You might invite someone from the local electric company to talk to the students.
3. Instruct students to design a poster sharing the information they learned about electricity. These posters should detail how electricity works and how to be safe around it. Post the posters in a school hallway to share the information with others.

Response Questions

Group Discussion Questions

- Have you ever had an experience with electricity that you would like to share?
- How has electricity changed people's lives? What would it be like to live without electricity?

Written Response Question

- What are all the different ways in which people use electricity today? What are some new inventions that have been discovered using electricity? How will our world continue to change as a result of electricity?

Name____________________________ Date ____________________

Picture the Process

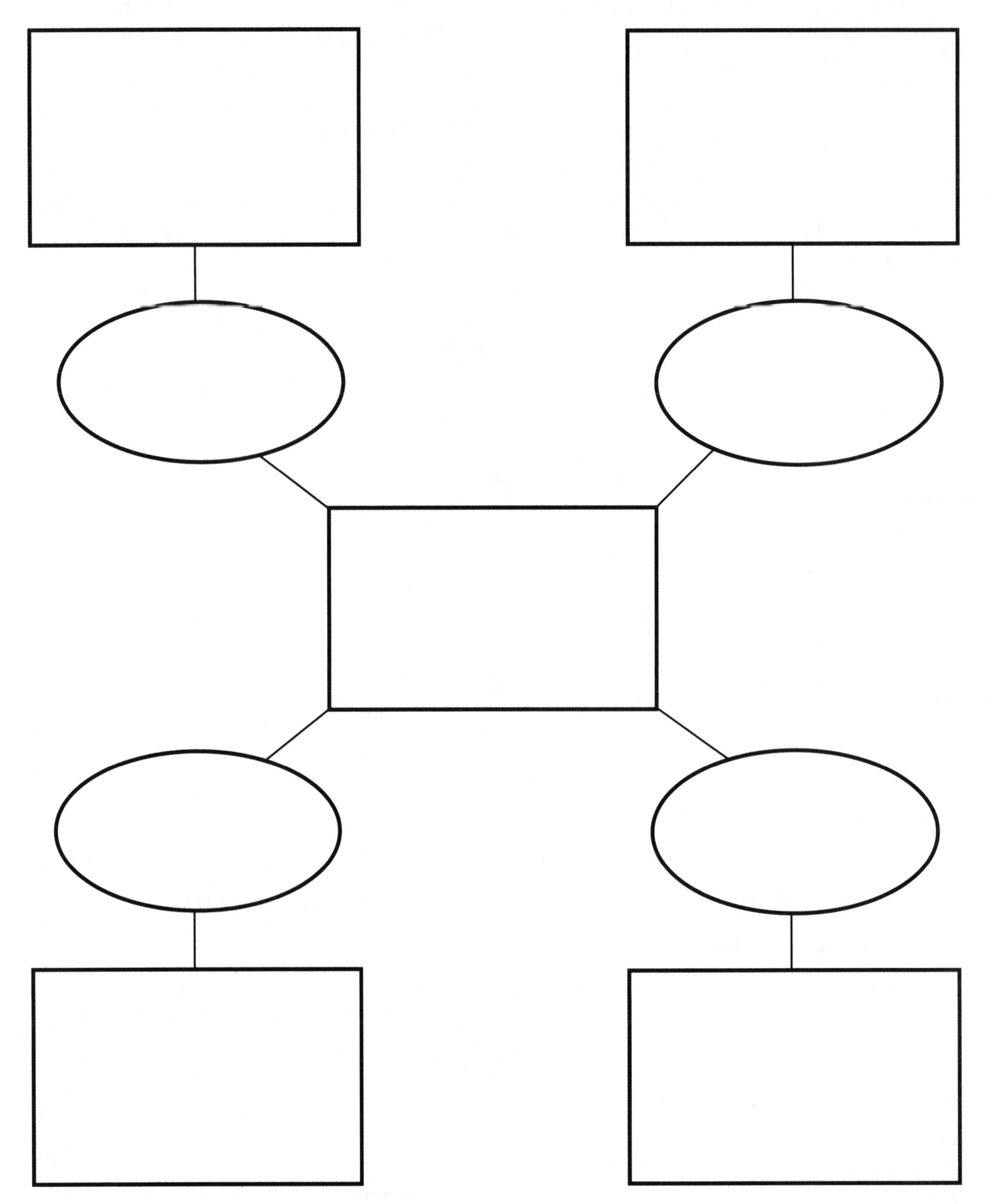

Electricity

By Sarah Kartchner Clark

A reader's theater with three parts

Reader 2: Hey! What is all around us and makes our modern lifestyle possible?

Reader 1: How about air?

Reader 2: Nope. Electricity.

Reader 3: What's that?

Reader 2: It's energy. You can find electricity everywhere.

Reader 1: Give me some examples of what you mean.

Reader 2: How about the lightning in the sky during a thunderstorm? The lightning is electricity.

Reader 3: Really?

Reader 2: Yes, and how about the electrical outlets in the house? Each outlet has electricity inside. We plug a cord in to connect to the electricity.

Reader 1: That's why you should never poke anything into an electrical outlet.

Reader 3: Is that all?

Reader 2: Oh no. Most batteries can produce different amounts of electricity. And how about when you drag your feet across the floor and then touch something? You know that shock? That's electricity, too.

Reader 3: Wow! So how does electricity work?

Electricity *(cont.)*

Reader 1: It begins with electrons. All atoms contain one or more electrons. The electrons carry a negative charge.

Reader 2: How do you know all this?

Reader 1: I've been to school, too.

Reader 2: Amazing! Let's keep going. Many atoms keep their electrons close. The electrons stick to the atoms.

Reader 1: These kinds of materials are called electrical insulators.

Reader 2: It basically means that these materials don't conduct electricity very well.

Reader 1: Examples of these materials are wood, plastic, glass, air, and cotton.

Reader 3: Are there materials that do conduct electricity?

Reader 2: Yes! Most metals have electrons that can separate from the atoms and move around. These electrons are called free electrons.

Reader 3: Does that mean that they didn't have to pay?

Reader 2: No, it means that they move around freely.

Reader 1: Some of the metals that conduct electricity are gold, silver, copper, aluminum, and iron.

Reader 2: The moving electrons transmit electrical energy from one point to another.

Reader 1: Electricity needs a conductor in order to move. It also needs something to take electricity through the conductor.

Reader 2: A generator uses a magnet to make the electrons move.

Electricity *(cont.)*

Reader 1: There is definitely a link between electricity and magnetism.

Reader 3: Getting too much electricity can be bad, right?

Reader 1: Yes. The static electricity isn't strong enough to hurt us, but we can be electrocuted by playing with electrical outlets or other forms of electricity.

Reader 2: Electricity can be transported along wire lines. You know those lines on the high poles?

Reader 3: Yes. So, why don't the birds, who sometimes sit on the wires, get electrocuted?

Reader 2: Because the birds are not touching the ground or any other grounded object.

Reader 1: If you or anything you are holding, like a metal ladder or pole, touches an electrical line, you become the electricity's conductor to the ground and you will be electrocuted.

Reader 3: Did Benjamin Franklin have something to do with electricity?

Reader 2: Yes. The story is that Ben Franklin attached an iron spike to a silk kite that he was flying during a thunderstorm, while holding the end of the kite with an iron key.

Reader 1: When the lightning flashed, a tiny spark jumped from the metal key to his wrist. It was a very dangerous experiment.

Reader 2: Can somebody turn on a light? It's getting dark in here!

Reader 2: One way to get electricity moving is to use a generator.

Reader 3: Electricity sounds very busy. It involves a lot of people and things.

References Cited

Kuhn, Melanie R. and Steven A. Stahl. 2000. *Fluency: A review of developmental and remedial practices*. Ann Arbor, MI: Center for the Improvement of Early Reading Achievement.

LaBerge, David and S. Jay Samuels. 1974. Toward a theory of automatic information processing in reading. *Cognitive Psychology* 6: 293–323.

National Reading Panel. 2000. *Teaching children to read: An evidence-based assessment of the scientific research literature on reading and its implications for reading instruction—reports of the subgroups.* Washington, DC: National Institute of Child Health and Human Development.

Rasinski, Timothy. 1990. *The effects of cued phrase boundaries in texts.* Bloomington, IN: ERIC Clearinghouse on Reading and Communication Skills.

Samuels, S. Jay. 1979. The method of repeated reading. *The Reading Teacher* 32: 403–408.

U.S. Department of Education. 2001. *Put Reading First: The Research Building Blocks for Teaching Children to Read.* Washington, DC: U.S. Government Printing Office.

Recommended Children's Literature

Cary, Barbara. *Meet Abraham Lincoln*. New York: Random House, 2001.

Curie, Eve. *Madame Curie: A Biography*. Cambridge, MA: De Capo Press, 2001.

Denenberg, Barry. *Early Sunday Morning: The Pearl Harbor Diary of Amber Billows, Hawaii, 1941*. New York: Scholastic, 2001.

Furniss, Tim. *A History of Space Exploration*. Guilford, CT: The Lyons Press, 2003.

Hesse, Karen. *Out of the Dust*. New York: Scholastic Press, 1997.

Kalman, Bobbie. *How a Plant Grows*. New York: Crabtree Publishing, 1996.

Parker, Steve. *Electricity*. New York: DK Cildren, 2005.

Petty, Ann. *Harriet Tubman: Conductor on the Underground Railroad*. Amistad Press, 1995.

Rostkowski, Margaret. *After the Dancing Days*. New York: HarperCollins, 1988.

Van Riper Jr., Guernsey. *Jim Thorpe: Olympic Champion*. New York: Aladdin, 1986.

van Rose, Susanna. *Volcanoe & Earthquake (DK Eyewitness Books)*. New York: DK Children, 2008.

Weitzman, David. *Model T: How Henry Ford Built a Legend*. New York: Crown Books for Young Readers, 2002.

Contents of the Teacher Resource CD

Script Title	Filename
The Assembly Line	assemblyline.pdf
World War I	worldwarI.pdf
The Great Depression	greatdepression.pdf
World War II	worldwarII.pdf
Jim Thorpe	jimthorpe.pdf
Abraham Lincoln	abrahamlincoln.pdf
Madame Marie Curie	madamemariecurie.pdf
Harriet Tubman	harriettubman.pdf
Earthquakes	earthquakes.pdf
Space Exploration	spaceexploration.pdf
Plant Life	plantlife.pdf
Electricity	electricity.pdf
Graphic Organizer	**Filename**
What's the Main Idea?	whatsthemainidea.pdf
K-W-L Chart	kwlchart.pdf
Main Idea	mainidea.pdf
Idea Web	ideaweb.pdf
Story Map	storymap.pdf
Cluster Web	clusterweb.pdf
Outline Form	outlineform.pdf
Compare and Contrast	compareandcontrast.pdf
Topic Diagram	topicdiagram.pdf
Comprehension Chart	comprehensionchart.pdf
Picture the Process	pictureprocess.pdf

Notes

Notes